**Body Toning: New Directions in
Women's Exercise
by Carrie Ogawa Wong**

**Body Toning: New Directions in Women's Exercise
by Carrie Ogawa Wong**

Copyright © 2025 I&I SPORTS SUPPLY. All rights reserved.
Published by I&I SPORTS SUPPLY
ISBN 978-1-326-64127-6

PROFILE

Carrie Ogawa was born on a small family farm in Osgood, Idaho. Being the oldest of three sisters, she carried many of the responsibilities and chores an older brother might assume as well as being mother's helper. Farming and caring for the livestock, which most cityfolk would consider a man's job, were all part of her daily work routine.

When Carrie was five years old, she was enrolled in a dance school where she studied classical ballet, jazz, and tap dancing. This was her first experience with formal exercise and it gave her an appreciation for movement, timing, grace, and coordination. The strength that she developed growing up on the farm naturally seemed to combine with the grace she acquired through her dancing, giving her a unique foundation when she began her training in the martial arts.

Carrie began her training in karate in 1975, obtaining a brown belt degree in two years. In 1977, she moved to California and joined the Sil Lum White Lotus Kung Fu Club under the direction of Douglas Wong. She competed in that same year and took first place among all the top black belt female competitors. Since then, she has won various Grand Championships in hand-form competitions and has also been rated as the number one weapons competitor.

Joining the national circuit of competitors, she went to Ogden, Utah, and took second place competing against both men and women. In Las Vegas, Nevada, she took first place in the women's division and came in as the second place runner up for the Grand Championship. Entering both hand-forms and weapon divisions in the Ed Parker Internationals in Long Beach, Carrie placed within the top three slots consecutively in 1978, 1979, 1980 and 1981. In 1981, Carrie competed in every major tournament on the West Coast as well as in the nationally rated tournament in Oklahoma City.

In 1980, the Inside Kung Fu Star Rating System classified Carrie as the eighth-ranked female competitor on the circuit. In 1981, Carrie moved up to second place in that system. In all other ranking systems, she has placed within the top ten.

In 1981, Carrie debuted on Los Angeles television in a "Tribute to Bruce Lee" special. She also performed at a major demonstration at the Tropicana Hotel with many of the top ranking masters and was included in a photo-spread in *Black Belt* magazine. Within a period of six years, Carrie has gained recognition as one of the top five female competitors in the United States.

Carrie is presently working for Unique Publications as well as teaching Kung-fu and women's exercise classes. Although she has not retired from competition, she is planning to concentrate on further developing women's fitness and self-defense programs.

TABLE OF CONTENTS

Acknowledgements 2

Dedication 3

Introduction 4

New Directions 7

Exercise Programs 8

   Beginner Programs 9

   Intermediate Programs 11

   Advanced Programs 14

Dynamic Tension 18

Proper Breathing 19

Stances 20

Upper Body Exercises 22

Waist and Hip Exercises 71

Lower Body (Legs) Exercises 113

Stretching Exercises 153

Advanced Stretching Exercises 211

Exercises With A Partner 228

Exercises With A Stick 240

Exercises With A Weighted Tin Can 257

Exercises With A Chair 273

Exercises With A Pillow 291

Summary 302

ACKNOWLEDGEMENT

I would like to thank the many wonderful people that have made this impossible task a reality. An idea that started from a single conversation has flourished into a lifelong dream come true.

To Mr. Curtis F. Wong for giving me the opportunity to write this book; to Mrs. Margie Tajiri for initiating this project; to Ms. Sandra Segal for helping to finalize the written portion of this text; to Mr. Ed Ikuta for the smooth-running photo sessions that produced such fabulous pictures; to Mr. Jeff Dungfelder for the excellent presentation and pictorial layout; to Ms. Kim Gallegos for the fine assistance as my training partner; to Mr. Daniel M. Furuya for the final evaluation and editing of this book and to the many people who have helped me behind the scenes.

I would especially like to thank my many wonderful teachers who have helped me throughout my career in dancing, cheerleading, karate and kung fu training. Thank you for the seeds you implanted into my mind. From these few seeds, many fruitful changes have flourished.

Last, but not least, to my husband and kung fu instructor as well, for showing me how to unite all of my training methods into one unit and then create my own specialized exercises.

DEDICATION

I would like to dedicate this book to my family. To my father, a man who always provided for the family and especially for me who spent countless hours on the job to make sure we were all taken care of, always fed and clothed, and who showed us strength and compassion while still disciplining us in the facts of the real world. To a wonderful mother who made sure that I could attend dancing classes by ironing clothes those many long hours while I practiced. Thank you for taking care of me when I was sick, for being there when I was happy, for supporting me when I undertook many impossible tasks and yet always remaining there to protect and love me. To my two sisters, Sherry and Geraldine, for the moral support whenever I needed it. Thank you for standing by me from the lowest of my days to the highest and happiest moments of my life.

A family is a unit in which the members can help or destroy each other. I was fortunate enough to have a very loving and understanding family. A family that stood together through the many obstacles of life but yet supported its members through the rough times and the good times. You can always turn to your family when everyone else gives up on you and a family is always there to make life a little easier. The love is the most important aspect of any family.

> Thank you for being there when I need you most.
> Thank you for being there in my happiest hours.
> Thank you for just being there!

INTRODUCTION

The modern, mechanized world conspires against letting us get the activity we need to keep our bodies healthy and in good shape. We have automatic doors, escalators, elevators, electric toothbrushes, and even electric pencil sharpeners, all of which keep us from ever having to use our own muscles. We drive to work and sit all day in front of an electric typewriter with an automatic correction device and—perhaps with a computerized memory! All the conveniences we live with are wonderful, but they make our bodies lazy and out of shape. Because of our lack of activity, our muscles lose their tone becoming flabby and weak.

Compare this world with the world of my parents. I was brought up on a farm until I was ten years old, and always got plenty of exercise chasing cows into corrals, climbing over and under fences, and working in the garden. Even running to the outhouse was good exercise! Both of my parents were extremely fit, as they did all the work themselves. I remember my father moving huge irrigation pipes by hand. Now there are automatic timed devices to do this work. In the fall, both of my parents would lift, throw, and stack bales of alfalfa, each of which weighed at least one hundred pounds. For my parents, both of whom are under five feet tall, this was some achievement! When potato harvest time came around, my parents would lift sacks of potatoes that weighed over one hundred pounds as if they were nothing. My mother was in such good physical condition that within one week of having a baby, she was back working in the fields. Today, I see women having a hard time lifting a five pound bag of sugar or even a small bag of groceries.

Not only does the mechanized, fast-paced world give us shapeless flabby bodies, but it also increases our problems with tension and stress. Today's women have multiple responsibilities. Many women have careers, as well as having all the responsibilities of mothers, wives, and homemakers. Women often follow an extremely tight schedule in which tension quickly builds up. Most of us don't have an opportunity to release this mental and physical strain while on the job. And when we get home, instead of exercising and stretching, we might try to unwind with a drink before falling into bed. This constant tension eventually causes migraines, high blood pressure, back problems, ulcers and a shorter life. Our outlook on life is affected and we become irritable with our family and co-workers. Even relatively young women begin to look old and drawn. There is no liveliness in their step or sparkle in their eyes. They look stiff and weak and feel tired all the time. Their whole outlook on life becomes negative and sometimes selfdestructive. Unfortunately, many women use this constant feeling of being sick as an excuse not to exercise when exercise would be the best thing for them.

What will a regular exercise program do to help? First, exercising regularly immediately helps you to release mental and physical stress. If you watch a small child when he gets upset, you will see that he lies down and has a tantrum for five minutes, kicking, crying, and hitting for all he's worth. Five minutes later, he's fine and walking away happily to play again. As an adult, you can't have a tantrum, and the tension builds up and up. However, it is vital to work off this stress, perhaps by running up the stairs or doing the filing. As you become involved in an exercise program, you will become more aware of the tension in your body and will be able to release this tension through exercises before it can build up to dangerous levels. You'll also be able to relax more easily, as exercised muscles can release tension more fully. You will sleep more deeply, and wake up more refreshed.

As you become physically fit and tone up your body, an exercise program will help improve your appearance. Bulges around the waist, flabby underarms, and sagging buttocks will disappear. Your body will have the smooth lines which come from muscle definition, instead of slack, dimpled flesh. When you gain in strength and flexibility in the lower back and legs, your posture will improve and you will avoid the hunched over look of the elderly and senile.

As you grow stronger, you will find you can become more independent. You will no longer have to wait for a man's help in order to move furniture or lift a water bottle. Carrying groceries will no longer be such a chore. You will have an increased store of energy and feel like going out dancing when you get home from work, instead of collapsing in front of the television or falling into bed. As you begin to feel better about yourself, and your tension is reduced, your attitude towards your work, family, and friends will also improve. You will be easier to get along with. You will find more meaning and satisfaction in your life.

As your body begins to firm up, clothes will begin to fit better. I went through this process recently. When I got tired of the same chubby body and began doing the exercises in the pages to come, I dropped ten pounds and shaped up my body through toning. Clothes that had sat in my closet for a year fit like a dream. Some were even too big! Everyone thought I splurged my money and bought an entirely new wardrobe.

I designed this exercise program specifically to reach all these goals while fitting into the lifestyle of the modern woman. Many of the exercises can be incorporated into your daily routine. You will find that you can use the "square horse" while doing dishes, fixing your hair, or cleaning the house. Stretching exercises can be done while watching television, working in the garden, or picking up around the house.

I have also tried to help prevent the exercise routine from becoming boring. I hear a lot of complaints about the boredom of the usual programs which repeat the same exercises over and over. To avoid boredom, I Ve included a huge range of exercises, and indicated which can be substituted for which. In the front of the book, there are several complete programs with many alternate exercises, or you can design your own program to work on specific parts of the body. There is also no pressure on you to keep up with a "Twenty-One Day Beautiful Body Plan." You will find that the exercises allow you to increase strength and flexibility at your own pace.

Most importantly, you will get immediate results from this program. I am currently teaching a woman's exercise class, which is made up of young women who were out of shape and stiff, older women who hadn't exercised in years, and even one woman with a back problem. All of them followed essentially the same program with variations tailored to fit each individual. By following the program only once or twice a week, within six months they all noticed a dramatic increase in flexibility and overall body toning. They increased in abdominal strength, their arms became less flabby and their leg muscles tightened. Many of the women found that their other activities became easier and noticed an increase in stamina and endurance. The program increased the range of motion for the woman with the back injury. In addition, many of the students lost weight, as well as losing inches at the waist. By following the program more consistently, either every other day, or, ideally, every day, you will get results even more quickly.

As your body begins to visibly improve, you will be motivated to continue exercising. Everyone—men as well as women—wants to look as good as they can. And anyone can have a beautiful body. But to look beautiful, takes work and dedication and the willingness to sweat and make sometimes painful demands on the body. However, as your work begins to quickly pay off in compliments and an improved self-image, you will be inspired to continue. Everyone can be healthy and beautiful!

NEW DIRECTIONS

Although sports and games have existed for centuries in the western world, the concept of systematic exercise is relatively new. The ancient Greeks explored physical discipline but this tradition was lost with the end of their empire and was rediscovered only in the last century. It is within the last several decades that modern science has directed its attention and efforts to this area of study. It is very likely that your parents never heard the terms *kinesiology, biokinetics* and *dynamic tension,* when they were attending school. All these terms refer to modern exercise and conditioning. Indeed, it is only within the last several years that we, ourselves, are finding out what they mean.

In the Orient, exercise and physical discipline has existed for over two thousand years. In the very early practices of Yoga based on the sacred texts of the Upanishads and the Patanjali through the origins of Chinese kung-fu created centuries before the birth of Christ, Oriental exercise in many forms has undergone a continuous tradition of refinement even to this very day. Western science has found great knowledge and inspiration in these disciplines which they have built upon in their "own" new sciences.

The exercises found in this book are modern exercises for the modern woman based on the ancient principles of Chinese kung-fu and inspired by the classical philosophy of the East. This book is not merely trying to be different or throw a new gimmick at you like many books. It is not like serving left-overs at the dinner table hidden under a new sauce. It is, by no means, a "re-hash." Through my studies and experiences, I have found these exercises to be the most appropriate and effective for today's women. Most of the common exercises that you know of today were originally designed for men. In ancient Greece, for example, exercises and games were practiced exclusively by men. It will be a few more years before we see women's football on television, I am sure. In ancient China, this restriction was never made. "Kung-fu," which is commonly known as Chinese martial arts, simply means "effort," "work" or "exercise." There was no restriction for women.

Today, in some cases, men's exercises have been adapted for women. In most cases, however, women have had to adapt themselves to the exercises. I really don't feel that this is a good working concept. The exercises I am presenting to you in this book were originally designed for both men and women. I find this quality and sense most appealing to me. Where I have found the traditional exercise a little dated, I have revised it or substituted a new, modern version always keeping you, the modern woman, in mind. As a result, I see a *new direction* forming in women's exercises. This is only the first step....

EXERCISE PROGRAMS

The following three complete exercise programs are designed to be used in progressive states of your development toward health and well being.

1) Beginning Program

This program systematically begins to strengthen and stretch all muscle groups of your body. If you're unable to execute the number of repetitions listed, do as many as you can. It is better to do a few exercises in each category than to only complete half of the program.

Do not overstrain yourself, but gradually add to the number of repetitions you do until you are doing the full amount required. Do not go beyond the number of reps listed. Rather, change to the next more advanced program. Instead of merely increasing reps (constant repetition can be a source of boredom), the more advanced programs substitute more advanced and strenuous exercises.

2) Intermediate Program

In the intermediate program, you will begin to find a list of alternative exercises which can be substituted for the more basic ones. These may not affect exactly the same muscle groups as the exercise for which they are substituted. However, by exercising similar but slightly different muscle groups, they increase the range and value of the program. These alternates may be added to the basic program in addition to being used as substitutes if you desire to lengthen and intensify the program.

3) Advanced Program

The advanced program provides very strenuous exercises and substitutes. As you increase in strength and flexibility you may alter the program to suit your needs by increasing your repetitions beyond the listed number at this level or by including and/or substituting the alternate exercise in your program. You may note that it is possible to construct a full exercise program from the alternate exercises themselves. Variety and alternating the exercises allows you to continue to challenge yourself with a wider range of activities.

BEGINNER'S PROGRAM

PROGRAM/EXERCISE	REPS	SUBSTITUTE/VARIATION
DYNAMIC TENSION		
Finger Thrust	3	Side Finger Thrust
		Front Finger Thrust
Side Lifts	3	Side Lift - Palms Up
Front and Back Press	3	Front & Back Press - Bent Arm
Dynamic Hand Grips	5	
Monk Hand	3	
WAIST		
Waist Rotations	3 each direction	
Waist Bends	3 each direction	
Arm Clasp Waist Twist	3 each direction	
Waist Bends - Reaching	3 each direction	
Hip Rotations	5 each direction	
Pelvic Thrusts	5 each direction	
Hip Lifts	5 each direction	
STOMACH		
Sit Up Against the Wall	5	
V-ups	5	
Sitting Twists	3 each direction	
LEGS		
Side Leg Lifts	5	
Side Leg Lifts - Inner Thigh	3 to 5	
Moon Walking	5 each leg	
Toe Raises	3-5 each position	

BEGINNER'S PROGRAM

PROGRAM/EXERCISE	REPS	SUBSTITUTE/VARIATION
STRETCHING		
ARMS - Arm Stretches	1 series	
Back of Wrist Stretch	1 series	
Shoulder Stretch	2 series	
LEGS - Standing Leg Stretch	3	
Hurdle Stretch	2 series	
Legs Extended Stretch	3	
Half Lotus	2 each direction	
Pancake Stretch	2 series	
Spread Leg Stretch	3 series	
BACK - Cobra Stretch	3	
Lower Back Stretch	2 series	
Lower Back Press	3	

INTERMEDIATE PROGRAM

PROGRAM/EXERCISE	REPS	SUBSTITUTE/VARIATION
DYNAMIC TENSION		
Finger Thrust	5	Finger Thrust Front and Side
Side Lifts	5	Side Lifts Alternating Palms
Front and Back Press	5	
Front and Back Thrust	5	
Dynamic Hand Grips	5	Dynamic Hand Grips Twisting
Monk Hand	5	Front and Back Monk Hand
WAIST		
Waist Rotations	5 each direction	Waist Rotations - Feet Together
Waist Bend	5 each direction	Waist Bend - Arch
Arm Clasp Waist Twist	5 each direction	
Waist Bends Reaching	5 each direction	Waist Bends Reaching - To Heel
Hip Rotations	5 each direction	
Pelvic Thrusts	5 each direction	
Hip Lift	5-7 each side	
Cross Chest Leg Lifts	3-5	
ABDOMEN		
Sit Up Against the Wall	10	Sit Up with Leg Press (CAN)
		Weighted Leg Lift (CAN)
Leg Lifts	3-5	Holding Can Leg Lifts (CAN)
		Leg Clap (CAN)
V-ups	5	Separated V-ups
		Holding Can Leg Lifts (CAN)
		Leg Tucks (PILLOW)
Sitting Twists	5 each direction	

INTERMEDIATE PROGRAM

PROGRAM/EXERCISE	REPS	SUBSTITUTE/VARIATION
LEGS		
Side Leg Lifts	5	Side Leg Lifts - Both Legs
Side Leg Lifts - Inner Thigh	5	Leg Press (PARTNER)
		Knee Press (CAN)
		Raised Inner Thigh (CHAIR)
		Buttocks Firmer (PILLOW)
		Concentrated Pillow Press (PILLOW)
Moon Walking	10	
Leg Squat	3-5	Knee Press (STICK)
Cross Leg Lift	3-5	
Toe Raises	5 each position	
STRETCHING		
ARMS - Arm Stretch	1 series	One Hand Twist (STICK)
Back of Wrists	1 series	Inside Out Wrist (STICK)
Shoulder Stretch	2 series	Shoulder Roll (STICK)
		Elbow Press (STICK)
LEGS - Leg Stretch Standing	3-5	Leg Stretch (CHAIR)
Leg Separated Stretch	3-5	Leg Stretch (CHAIR)
Hurdle Stretch	3 series	Phoenix Stretch (ADVANCED STRETCHING)
		Leg Stretch (CHAIR)

INTERMEDIATE PROGRAM

PROGRAM/EXERCISE	REPS	SUBSTITUTE/VARIATION
Hurdle Stretch Back	3	
Legs Extended Stretch	3	
Half Lotus	2 each direction	
Spread Leg Stretch	3 series	Leg Extension (ADVANCED STRETCHING)
		Leg Lift Pulling (ADVANCED STRETCHING)
		Chinese Splits (ADVANCED STRETCHING)
		Leg Swings (CHAIR)
Inner Thigh Stretch	3 series	Twisting Thigh Stretch
Split Preparation	3 series	Advanced Splits (ADVANCED STRETCHING)
		Split Stretch (PARTNER STRETCHING)
BACK - Cobra Stretch	3-5	
Lower Back Stretch	3 series	
Lower Back Press	5	

ADVANCED PROGRAM

PROGRAM/EXERCISE	REPS	SUBSTITUTE/VARIATION
DYNAMIC TENSION		
Finger Thrust	5	Finger Thrust Front and Side Body Lift (CHAIR)
Tucked Rotation	5	
Side Lifts Alternating Palms	5	Side Lift - 45° Turn
Front and Back Thrust	5	Body Lift (CHAIR)
Dynamic Hand Grip Twisting	5	Dynamic Hand Grip Twisting - Arms Extended
Front and Back Monk Hand	5	
Monk Hand Twisting	5	
WAIST		
Waist Rotations	5 each direction	Waist Rotations - Feet Together
Waist Bend - Arching	5 each direction	Waist Bend 45°
Arm Clasp Waist Twist	5 each direction	
Waist Bends Reaching	5 each direction	Waist Bend Reaching - To Heel
Hip Rotations	5 each direction	
Pelvic Thrusts	5 each direction	
Hips Lifts	7-10 each side	
Cross Chest Leg Lifts	5-10 each side	

ADVANCED PROGRAM

PROGRAM/EXERCISE	REPS	SUBSTITUTE/VARIATION
ABDOMEN		
Sit Up Against the Wall	10	Twisted Sit Up
		Sit Up (PARTNER)
		Sit Up with Leg Press (CAN)
		Weighted Leg Lift (CAN)
Waist Crunch	5 each side	Raised Side Crunch (CAN)
		Side Crunch (CHAIR)
Sit Up - Abdominals Only	7-10	Sits Ups Holding Can (CAN)
		Double Knee Lift (CHAIR)
		Layered Sit Up (PILLOW)
Scissored Leg Lifts	7-10	Leg Clap (CAN)
		Leg Clap (CHAIR)
Side to Side Leg Lifts	5-10	Side to Side Leg Lifts - Legs Extended
Separated V-ups	5-10	Holding Can Leg Lifts (CAN)
		Leg Tucks (PILLOW)
Sitting Twists	5 each direction	
LEGS		
Side Leg Lifts - Both Legs	5-10	Side Leg Lift - Scissoring
Side Leg Lifts - Inner Thigh	5-10	Leg Press (PARTNER)
		Knee Press (CAN)
		Raised Inner Thigh (CHAIR)
		Buttocks Firmer (PILLOW)
		Concentrated Pillow Press (PILLOW)
Moon Walking	10	
Leg Squat	5-10	Knee Press (STICK)
Cross Leg Lift	7-10	
Toe Raises	5 each position	

ADVANCED PROGRAM

PROGRAM/EXERCISE	REPS	SUBSTITUTE/VARIATION
STRETCHING		
ARMS - Arm Stretch	1-2 series	One Hand Twist (STICK)
Back of Wrists	1-2 series	Inside Out Wrist (STICK)
Shoulder Stretch	1-2 series	Shoulder Roll (STICK)
		Elbow Press (STICK)
LEGS - Leg Stretch Standing	5	Leg Stretch (CHAIR)
Leg Separated Stretch	5	Leg Stretch (CHAIR)
Hurdle Stretch	3-5 series	Phoenix Stretch (ADVANCED STRETCHING)
		Leg Stretch (CHAIR)
Hurdle Stretch Back	3-5 series	
Legs Extended Stretch	3-5	
Half Lotus	2 each direction	
Tucked Hurdle Stretch	3 each direction	
Cross Knees	3-5 each direction	
Spread Leg Stretch	3-5 series	Leg Extension (ADVANCED STRETCHING)
		Leg Lift Pulling (ADVANCED STRETCHING)
		Chinese Splits (ADVANCED STRETCHING)
		Groin Press Stretch (PARTNER)
		Leg Swings (CHAIR)

ADVANCED PROGRAM

PROGRAM/EXERCISE	REPS	SUBSTITUTE/VARIATION
Inner Thigh Stretch	3 series	Twisting Thigh Stretch
Split Preparation	3 series	Advanced Splits (ADVANCED STRETCHING)
		Split Stretch (PARTNER STRETCHING)
Hip Stretch	3-5	Foot Behind Neck (ADVANCED STRETCH)
BACK - Cobra Stretch	5	
Lower Back Stretch	5 series	
Lower Back Press	5	

DYNAMIC TENSION

Dynamic tension pits one muscle against another. As an example, push your palms together as if trying to keep someone from pulling them apart. Feel the tension in the upper arms and lateral area. This tension develops your strength without any loss of flexibilty.

This method is preferable to exercises using weights or a Nautilus machine for several reasons: no apparatus is required; there is no danger of overstraining your body by using excessive weights; and your strength builds up gradually and naturally, since you automatically and naturally increase the tension involved in each exercise as you grow stronger. Dynamic tension also has the advantage of developing complete muscle groups rather than concentrating on a single muscle such as the biceps in the arms which is common in many weight-training exercises.

Dynamic tension is ideal for strengthening and toning muscles regardless of your level of fitness when you begin the program. This makes dynamic tension particularly good for women who are often discouraged when they begin a strengthening program finding that even the lightest weight is too strenuous. Women also find that dynamic tension exercises allow them to firm body areas such as the underarms which is difficult even with advanced weight training programs.

In dynamic tension, muscle tone is achieved without any loss of flexibility. The steady push of dynamic tension pumps your muscles full of blood, then stretches them as they relax. This steady stretch prevents the shortening of muscles that is caused by the short, jerky motions of many weight-lifting or calisthenic programs.

Dynamic tension exercises can be easily incorporated into your daily lifestyle. Once you are familiar with the principles of dynamic tension, you can exercise your muscles while you are driving, watching television or at work. As you advance in this program, you may wish to add weights to your dynamic tension routine to enhance the strengthening affects further. This will be explained in a later chapter.

PROPER BREATHING

Muscles need large quantities of energy because of the tremendous amount of work they do each day simply moving and supporting the body and its limbs. In order to gain energy, the muscles need oxygen. When you inhale, you take oxygen into your body which is transferred via the blood system to the muscles. Since your muscles need more nourishment when they are working, correct breathing is vital during an exercise program. Correct breathing also helps you relax your body while stretching.

Your breathing should be concentrated in the lower abdominal region. The method we will be using is a Chinese taoist method. When you inhale, you concentrate on directing air to an area three inches below the naval in what is called the "tan tien." This area is your center of gravity. Breathe through the nose with the tongue pushed to the roof or top of the mouth. Keep the mouth closed while inhaling and exhaling. Keeping the tongue on the roof of the mouth, you make sure that you inhale only through the nose. (You will find it almost impossible to inhale through the mouth with the tongue in this position.) This tongue position also keeps your mouth moist, so that it does not become uncomfortably dry as you exercise. Keep your breathing slow, steady, and regulated.

During the exercise, inhale at the maximum point of strength and exhale as the maximum point of exertion is reached. For example, when doing sit ups, inhale while lying back and exhale while sitting up. When you inhale and hold your breath, your body becomes tight and tense. If you try to exert yourself when you are tight in this way, you will find you are working against yourself. If you exhale when you reach the point of maximum exertion, your body will be more relaxed and move more efficiently.

During the exercises, you will be breathing regularly and very slowly. This is actually the way you naturally breathe when you are asleep and in your most relaxed state. Breathing in this way helps you keep your muscles from tensing up as you perform each exercise. Breathing also reduces stress.

This method of breathing should be incorporated into your everyday activities. For example, many women do not know how to lift heavy, awkward items correctly. They will use their backs in lifting objects which puts a dangerous strain on the vertabrae and lower back. Women often will inhale and hold their breath as they attempt to lift an object. As explained earlier, this causes the body to fight against itself. The correct way of lifting a heavy object is to use the legs and exhale slowly as you lift.

When learning to breathe correctly, pay close attention to your posture. Keep your back straight, head erect, and hips tucked under so as to keep a clear pathway for the air. Correct posture and breathing patterns will be covered in detail for each exercise.

STANCES

Square Horse

The "square horse" (Ma Pu) is a basic Chinese stance used in strengthening and stablilizing the lower portion of the body, especially the legs. The effects of this stance are concentrated on the inner and outer thigh, front (quadriceps) and back (bicep femoris) thigh, knees, calves, ankles, hips, buttocks and lower back.

The width of the stance will vary according to a person's size and flexibility. The square horse becomes wider and lower as you become more flexible. In the beginning, determine the square horse as follows: (1) Place feet together, turning the toes out but keeping the heels stationary. (2) Keeping the toes at this point, push the heels out. (3) The toes are again pushed out with the heels stationary. (4) The last foot movement is to push the heels out so both feet are now pointed straight ahead and parallel to each other. The weight is evenly distributed with the knees bent directly over the toes. Press the thighs out. Make sure the heels are pushed out at all times so the feet are parallel. Do not let the feet roll or tip sideways. The back must be kept straight. Align the top of your head directly over the tailbone and tuck your hips under. As you gain strength and flexibility in the legs; work on lowering the stance to the point where both thighs are parallel to the floor.

When you first start using this stance, you will probably feel uncomfortable. Your legs will ache, burn, and shake to some extent. This is normal for any beginner. You are placing the legs in a position to which your muscles are not accustomed, especially if you have not been very active or involved yourself in any exercise program. All of your weight is supported by the legs.

Use this "square horse" position whenever possible. Try to stay in a "square horse" in any of the exercises where you are stationary and concentrating on the upper body. In this way, you® lower body is exercising although you are not concentrating on it. No time is wasted in your exercise routine. You will find that if you are intensly concentrating on another exercise or body part, you won't be aware of any discomfort in the legs.

CONCENTRATION: Inner thigh, outer thigh, front thigh, back thigh, knees, calves, ankles, hips, buttocks, lower back.

Inward Horse

The "Inward Horse" is a variation of the square horse. (1) Begin with feet together. (2) Turn the toes out, leaving the heels stationary. (3) Then leave the toes stationary while swinging the heels out. (4) Feet should now be shoulder width apart with toes pointing inward. From this position, bend the knees, forcing together the thigh area from the knees to the crotch. Keep the hips tucked under with the back and head erect. This particularly helps strengthen the hips and lower back area.

As you become more comfortable in this position, spread the feet slightly further apart. This causes the stance to become lower and puts more pressure on the thighs.

CONCENTRATION: Thighs, hip area, lower back, knees and ankles.

UPPER BODY EXERCISES

FINGER THRUST

Stance

Beginner: Stand with legs shoulder width apart. Intermediate: Square Horse. Advanced: Square Horse.

Description

Begin with the arms tucked in at the sides. Hands are at shoulder height with the palms facing down. Exhaling, press the hands out with dynamic tension (using one muscle against another) leading with the fingertips. Halfway out, pull the fingertips back. Continue pressing with the palms, facing away from the body, until the arms have reached their full extension. Pull the arms to the front, palms remaining away from the body until they are almost touching. While inhaling, bend the elbows dropping the palms down and pull them tightly into the body. Move the hands and arms to the starting position to shoulder height with the arms tucked in at the sides.

Posture

The back should be kept straight; the hips tucked under, the head up and looking forward.

Remarks

As you press the arms out, you may hear a popping sound in the elbows or joints, this is usually caused by tight muscles. This popping sound is quite normal on the first repetition. Continued popping may be due to a prior injury in the elbow.

Remember to pull the wrists back until hands are at right angles to the forearms. Keep the fingers together and the thumbs tucked down. The shoulders are relaxed.

Concentration

Biceps, triceps, forearms, pectorals, shoulders and wrists.

FINGER THRUST

1

2

3

4

FINGER THRUST

5

6

7

8

SIDE FINGER THRUST

Stance

Square Horse

Description

Begin with the arms tucked in at the sides; the hands are shoulder height and the palms are facing down. Exhaling, press the hands out with dynamic tension leading with the fingertips. Halfway out, pull the fingertips back and continue pressing with the palms facing away from the body until the arms have reached their full extension. Inhaling, bend the elbows and pull the arms in with the palms facing away from the body. Halfway in, drop the palms down facing the floor. Continue pulling in until the arms are tucked in at the sides. The hands should now be in their original position.

Remarks

By not continuing the stretching motion forward to the front, this exercise concentrates on strengthening the lateral muscles.

Remember to pull the wrists back until the hands are at right angles to the forearms. Keep the fingers together and the thumbs tucked down. This will concentrate on the biceps, triceps, and forearms. Make sure that this exercise is done with the arms directly to the sides of the body. The shoulders are kept relaxed throughout this entire movement.

Concentration

Biceps, triceps, elbows, forearms, pectorals, shoulders, laterals and the wrists.

SIDE FINGER THRUST

1

2

3

SIDE FINGER THRUST

4

5

6

FRONT FINGER THRUST

Stance

Square Horse

Description

The hands are shoulder height in front of your chest and the palms are facing down. The right hand is in front of the right shoulder; the left hand is in front of the left shoulder. Exhaling, press the hands out with dynamic tension leading with the fingertips. Halfway out, pull the fingertips back. Continue pressing with the palms facing away from the body until the arms reach their extension. Inhaling, bend the elbows pulling the arms in with the palms facing away from the body. Halfway in, drop the palms down facing the floor and continue pulling in until the arms are tucked in front of each shoulder again. Press the hands out to the sides with the hands at shoulder height.

Remarks

By pulling the laterals forward, this exercise stretches as well as strengthens the shoulders.

Remember to pull the wrists back until the hands are at right angles to the forearms.

Concentration

Biceps, triceps, elbows, forearms, pectorals, shoulders and the wrists.

FRONT FINGER THRUST

1

2

3

FRONT FINGER THRUST

4

5

6

COMBINED FINGER THRUSTS

Stance

    Square Horse

Description

    Combine the side and front finger thrust into one continuous series of movements. Begin with the arms tucked in at the sides, the hands are at shoulder height and the palms are facing down. Exhaling, press the hands out with dynamic tension leading with fingertips. Halfway out, pull the fingertips back and continue pressing with the palms facing away from the body until the arms have reached their full extension. Inhaling, bend the elbows, pulling the arms in with the palms facing away from the body. Halfway in, drop the palms down facing the floor and continue pulling in until the arms are tucked in at the sides. The hands should now be in their original position.

    Move the hands forward until the right hand is in front of the right shoulder, the left hand is in front of the left shoulder. Press the hands out with dynamic tension leading with the finger tips. Halfway out pull the fingertips back. Continue pressing with the palms facing away from the body until the arms have reached their full extension. Inhaling, bend the elbows, pulling the arms in with the palms facing away from the body. Halfway in, drop the palms down facing the floor and continue pulling in until the arms are tucked in front of each shoulder. Press the hands out to the sides with the hands at shoulder height.

Remarks

    Pay attention as you do the transition movement from the side to the front and front to side working with the shoulders, laterals and the pectorals. While moving from the sides to the front, concentrate the dynamic tension to the lateral region. After completing the front thrust and moving to the sides, again concentrate on the lateral and shoulder region. Press the shoulder blades towards each other to stretch the frontal chest region.

    Remember to pull the wrists back until the hands are at right angles to the forearms.

COMBINED FINGER THRUSTS

1

2

3

4

COMBINED FINGER THRUSTS

5

6

7

8

TUCKED ROTATION

Stance

    Square Horse

Description

    Begin with the arms tucked in at the sides with hands at shoulder height and the palms down. Begin by inhaling. Then, exhaling, move the arms and hands forward with the right hand in front of right shoulder, the left hand in front of left shoulder using dynamic tension. Inhaling; move the arms and hands back so the arms are tucked at sides and the hands are shoulder height. Bring your arms to the sides and relax.

Remarks

    As in the side-front thrust, concentrate the dynamic tension in the lateral region while moving from the side to front position. While moving to the sides, concentrate on the lateral and shoulder region. Pressing the shoulder blades towards each other will also stretch the frontal chest region. Keep the shoulders down and relaxed.

Concentration

    Biceps, triceps, shoulders, pectorals, laterals and the wrists.

1   2

TUCKED ROTATION

3

4

5

SIDE LIFTS

Stance

    Beginner: Stand with the legs shoulder width apart. Intermediate: Square Horse. Advanced: Square Horse.

Description

    Begin with the arms straight along the sides of the body with the palms inward. Lift the arms upward using dynamic tension with the palms still facing down. Lift the arms to an overhead position until the backs of the hands touch. Then, pull the arms down to the starting position along the sides of your body using dynamic tension.

Posture

    Keep the shoulders relaxed and pressed back as you lift the arms up. Do not let the shoulders rise up towards the ears.
    Keep your back straight and the hips tucked under. The head should be erect and facing forward.

Breathing

    Normal, regulated breathing throughout the exercise.

Remarks

    Because this exercise uses the shoulder's full range of motion, you may hear clicking or grinding noises if the joints are tight.
    If you have tightened the muscles in your shoulder and upper back through other exercises you may find it difficult to press your hands together over your head. As you continue practicing this exercise, you will eventually gain the necessary flexibility.
    Keep the head erect and arms extended straight throughout the exercise.

Concentration

    Biceps, triceps, forearms, pectorals, shoulders and the laterals.

SIDE LIFTS

1

2

3

SIDE LIFTS

4

5

6

SIDE LIFTS - PALMS UP

Stance

    Square Horse

Description

    Begin with the arms straight along the sides with the palms turned away from the body. Lift the arms upward, focusing on dynamic tension with the palms facing up. Lift them to an overhead position where the palms of the hands will touch. Then pull the arms down to the starting position with the palms facing up.

Breathing

    Normal, regulated breathing throughout the exercise.

Remarks

    This variation concentrates on the full rotation of the shoulder joints while stretching and elongating the muscles of the upper arms. This exercise is especially good for under arms.
    Keep the shoulders relaxed and pressed back as you lift the arms.
    Keep your back straight, hips tucked under and the head erect with the arms extended straight throughout the entire exercise.

Concentration

    Biceps, triceps, forearms, pectorals, shoulders and the laterals.

SIDE LIFTS ■ PALMS UP

1

2

SIDE LIFTS - PALMS UP

3

4

5

SIDE LIFT • ALTERNATING PALM POSITION

Stance

    Square Horse

Description

    Begin with the arms straight along the sides with the palms turned toward the body. Lift the arms upward with dynamic tension with the palms facing down. Lift to an overhead position where the backs of the hands touch. Turn the palms so they are facing towards each other, then pull them down to the starting position with the palms facing up. Keep the palms facing up and lift to an overhead position where the palms touch. Turn the palms away from each other so they are now facing down. Then pull the arms down to the starting position.

Breathing

    Normal, regulated breathing throughout the exercise.

Remarks

    This exercise combines the benefits of the first two exercises. Be particularly careful to keep the shoulders relaxed throughout this series.
    Remember to keep the head erect and arms extended straight.

Concentration

    Biceps, triceps, forearms, shoulders and the laterals.

1

2

3

SIDE LIFT - ALTERNATING PALM POSITION

4

5

6

SIDE LIFT ■ FORTY-FIVE DEGREE TURNS

Stance

    Square Horse

Description

    Begin with the arms straight along the sides with the palms turned away from the body. Lift the arms upward using dynamic tension with the palms facing up. Continue to lift the arms to an overhead position until the palms of the hands touch. Turn the palms away from each other so the backs of the hands are touching and pull them down using dynamic tension. When the arms are approximately forty-five degrees from the overhead position, rotate your arms until the palms are facing upward. Then continue pulling them down to the sides of your body. Turn the hands over and you are ready to begin another series.

Breathing

    Normal, regulated breathing thoughout the exercise.

Remarks

    Be sure to keep the back straight with your head up and facing forward. When you turn the palms over at the forty-five degree position, your body will naturally begin to tip slightly. Concentrate on keeping your back straight. The shoulders must be relaxed so they gain full rotation of movement. Keep the arms straight.

Concentration

    Biceps, triceps, forearms, shoulders and laterals.

SIDE LIFT - FORTY-FIVE DEGREE TURNS

i

2

3

4

5

6

7

8

FRONT - BACK PRESS

Stance

Beginner: Stand with the legs shoulder width apart. Intermediate: Square Horse. Advanced: Square Horse.

Description

Inhaling, push the hands together in front of the body. The hands are at shoulder height with the arms locked straight out. Press the arms together hard using dynamic tension. Hold the breath down in the lower abdomen or "tan tien."^^ Exhale and relax the arms. Inhaling, move the arms to the back with hands pushing together. Try to lift the hands as far up the back as possible without resting the arms heavily on the back. The fingertips should be pointed down. Press hard using dynamic tension. Hold the breath down in the lower abdomen. Exhale and relax the arms.

Posture

The back should be kept straight (especially when the hands are behind the back), the hips are tucked under, the head is erect and facing forward. Keep the shoulders relaxed at all times.

Remarks

The further you move your hands away from the body, the more you force your muscles to exert effort. Therefore, if you feel excessive strain in the pectoral muscles while practicing this exercise, you may wish to work with a variation or alternative exercise until you are stronger.

When you press your hands together behind your back, you may feel a great deal of stress in the pectoral and shoulder muscles. This is natural because these muscles are seldom stretched out.

Concentration

Biceps, triceps, forearms, pectorals, shoulders, laterals and wrists.

FRONT - BACK PRESS

1

2

3

FRONT - BACK PRESS

4

5

6

FRONT - BACK BENT-ARM PRESS

Stance

    Square Horse

Description

    Begin with the arms extended halfway out, the hands are pressed together. Inhaling, push the hands together in front of the solar plexis region using dynamic tension. Hold the breath down in the lower abdomen. Exhale and relax the arms. Inhaling, move the arms behind your back with the hands pushing together. Again, bend the arms extending them halfway out behind you. Hold the breath down in the lower abdomen. Exhale and relax the arms.

Remarks

    This variation relieves some of the strain from the pectoral and shoulder muscles. However, since it allows you to press your arms together with greater force, it concentrates on developing the muscles in the upper and lower arms.

    Keep the back straight especially when the hands are pressed behind the back. Keep the shoulders relaxed.

Concentration

    Biceps, triceps, forearms, pectorals and shoulders.

FRONT - BACK BENT-ARM PRESS

1

2

3

FRONT ■ BACK THRUST

Stance
Square Horse

Description
Inhale, press the hands together in front of the solar plexus region. Exhaling, push the hands forward leading with the fingertips using dynamic tension. Keep pressing the hands together until the arms are extended straight forward and the elbows are locked. Inhaling, bend the elbows and pull the hands back while pressing them together. Continue pulling the hands back until you return to the starting position in front of the solar plexus. Relax the arms and move them behind your back. Inhale as you start with the hands pressed together and lift them up the back as far as possible with fingertips pointing down. Do not rest the arms heavily on the back. Exhaling, push the hands down and away from the back while pressing the hands together. Inhaling, pull the hands as far up the back as possible to the starting position. Exhale and relax the arms.

Remarks
Note that it becomes more difficult to maintain tension in your arms as you push the hands out. The outward movement stretches the muscles which are built up through dynamic tension.

Keep the back straight, shoulders relaxed, and the head erect.

Concentration
Biceps, triceps, forearms, pectorals, laterals and the shoulders.

1

2

3

4

FRONT - BACK THRUST

5

6

7

8

DYNAMIC HAND GRIPS

Stance

Beginning: Square Horse. Intermediate: Square Horse. Advanced: Square Horse.

Description

Begin with the arms bent and hands in clenched fists. Your elbows should be held the distance of at least one fist from the body. Inhale, holding the air down in the lower abdomen. Tighten up the entire upper torso using dynamic tension. Exhale, relax and then repeat.

Posture

Keep the back straight, the hips tucked in and the head erect and looking forward.

Make sure that your heels are pushed out, the feet are parallel and the knees are over the toes while maintaining the square horse stance. When you assume the square horse, concentrate on lowering your hips as far down as possible.

Remarks

Don't hold yourself tightly or hold your breath for a long period of time putting undue stress on your heart.

Concentration

Biceps, triceps, forearms, pectorals, shoulders, laterals, abdomen and the lower body.

DYNAMIC HAND GRIPS

1

2

DYNAMIC HAND GRIPS - TWISTING

Stance

   Square Horse

Description

   Begin with the arms bent and the hands in a fisted position. The fists are facing up. Your elbows should be held the distance of at least one fist from the body. Inhale, hold the air down in the lower abdomen. Tighten up all of your upper torso muscles using dynamic tension and simultaneously rotate the fists so they now face down. Exhale and relax the body while maintaining the same position of the fists. Inhale, holding the air down in the lower abdomen. Tighten up all of the upper torso muscles and simultaneously rotate the fists to the starting position so they face up this time. Exhale, relax and repeat.

Remarks

   This exercise focuses on increasing the range of motion in the shoulders while working all the upper body muscles.

Concentration

   Biceps, triceps, forearms, pectorals, shoulders, laterals, abdomen and lower body.

DYNAMIC HAND GRIPS - TWISTING

1

2

3

4

DYNAMIC HAND GRIPS - EXTENDED

Stance

    Square Horse

Description

    Begin with the arms extended in front of the body with your fists facing up. Inhale, holding the air down in the lower abdomen. Tighten up all of the upper torso muscles using dynamic tension and simultaneously rotate the arms so the fists are now facing down. Exhale, relax the body while maintaining the position of the fists. Inhale, holding the air down in the lower abdomen. Tighten up all of the upper torso muscles using dynamic tension and simultaneously rotate the fists to the starting position. The fists are now facing up. Exhale, relax and repeat.

Remarks

    This exercise also includes rotation of the shoulder joints but intensifies the tension on the muscles of the extended arms. Be sure to keep them straight. Keep the back straight, the head erect and the shoulders relaxed.

    Bend the knees as low as possible in the square horse position with the heels pushed out and the knees pointed over the toes.

Concentration

    Biceps, triceps, forearms, pectorals, shoulders, laterals, abdomen and lower body.

DYNAMIC HAND GRIPS - EXTENDED

1

2

3

4

MONK'S HAND

Stance
Beginner: Inward Horse. Intermediate: Inward Horse. Advanced: Inward Horse

Description
Begin with the hands pushing together and the elbows bent, as if praying with the fingertips pointing upwards. Push the hands together using dynamic tension. Simultaneously turn the hands down and hold briefly. As you continue pushing the hands together using dynamic tension, turn the hands up and then in towards the body. The fingertips should be pointed in at the solar plexus. Hold this position briefly. Leaving the left hand turned in, turn the right hand up and then away from the body. The right and left hands point in the opposite direction. Grasp the fingers of the right hand with the left hand in a pulling motion using dynamic tension. The right palm should be facing you and the left palm facing away from the body. Lift the arms and hands to the overhead position until the arms are locked. Pull down while still grasping the fingers and return to the starting position. Do not allow the elbows to rise.

Posture
Keep the shoulders relaxed especially when lifting the hands overhead. Keep your feet flat on the ground, hips tucked and the back straight. It is important that the head remain in the erect position looking forward throughout the exercise. Make sure legs are pressed together.

Remarks
Because of tightness in your shoulder muscles you may find it difficult to extend the hands overhead. The needed flexibility will come as you continue to practice the exercise. A clicking sound in the shoulders is caused by stiffness in the shoulder joints. Remember not to tip the head forward when the arms are stretched upward.

Breathing
Normal, regulated breathing throughout the exercise.

Concentration
Biceps, triceps, forearm, elbow, fingers, shoulders, pectorals, laterals and lower body.

MONK'S HAND

1

2

3

4

MONK'S HAND

5

6

7

8

FRONT AND BACK MONK'S HAND

Stance

    Inward Horse

Description

    Begin with the hands pushing together and the elbows bent with the fingertips pointing upwards as if praying like a monk. Push the hands together using dynamic tension. Simultaneously turn the hands down and hold them briefly. As you continue pushing the hands together using dynamic tension, turn the hands up and then inwards the body. Do not allow the elbows to rise. The fingertips should be pointed in at the solar plexus. Hold this position briefly. Leaving the left hand turned in, turn the right hand up and then away from the body. The right and left hands then point in the opposite direction. Grasp the fingers of the right hand with the left hand in a pulling motion using dynamic tension. The right palm should be facing you and the left palm facing away from the body. Lift the arms and hands to the overhead position until the arms are locked. Move the arms back and lower the grasped hands behind the back of the neck. The arms are relaxed. Hold this position, keep the head up and look forward as much as possible. Use your right hand to pull on the left arm and hand, so you slowly stretch the shoulder area and laterals. Reverse the direction and pull the right arm and hand with the left. You may want to do this several times to further loosen this area. Reposition the hands behind the neck. Grasping your fingers, use dynamic tension to lift the arms overhead and continue down in front to the starting position.

Remarks

    When repeating this exercise, alternate the position of your hands. For instance, on the second series leave the right hand turned in and turn the left hand so the fingers are pointing out. When grasping the fingers using dynamic tension, the left palm will be facing yourself and the right palm will be facing away.

    As your flexibility increases, try to increase your behind-the-back stretch until your hands reach your shoulders.

Posture

    Keep your back straight and head erect when stretching your shoulder area with the hands locked behind your head.

Concentration

    Bicep, tricep, forearm, elbow, fingers, shoulders, pectorals, laterals and lower body.

FRONT AND BACK MONK'S HAND

1

2

3

4

FRONT AND BACK MONK'S HAND

5

6

7

8

MONK HAND TWISTING

Stance

Inward Horse

Description

Begin with the hands pushing together with elbows bent and with fingertips pointing upwards as if praying. Push the hands together using dynamic tension. Simultaneously turn the hands down and hold them there briefly. As you continue pushing the hands together using dynamic tension, turn the hands upwards and then inwards to the body. Do not allow the elbows to rise. The fingertips should be pointed in at the solar plexus. Hold this position briefly. Leaving the left hand turned in, turn the right hand up and then away from the body. The right and left hand point in opposite directions.

Instead of grasping your fingers, continue rotating your hands in opposite directions. As the right hand turns out, the left hand turns in and vice versa. Maintain constant pressure using dynamic tension.

Remarks

The shoulders should be relaxed, keep the feet flat on the ground and the legs pressed together.

This exercise concentrates on the rotation of the wrists while applying dynamic tension. This improves flexibility in addition to strength.

Concentration

Biceps, triceps, forearms, wrists, pectorals and laterals.

MONK HAND TWISTING

1

2

3

4

WAIST AND HIP EXERCISES

WAIST ROTATIONS

Stance

Feet are shoulder width apart.

Description

Warm up slowly rotating your waist in a circle at your own pace, then reverse the direction. This loosens up the hips and lower back.

Put your hands on your hips. Bend forward until chest is parallel to the ground. Your back is slightly arched and your head is looking straight forward. Keeping your legs locked and your lower body stationary, slowly roll your body to the right until your right side is parallel to the ground. Keep your upper body in line with your lower body to obtain the maximum stretch of your left waist muscles. Next roll your body backwards. Arch your back as if beginning a back bend and let your head fall backwards. This stretches the abdominal muscles and lower back. Continue rolling to the left side, holding the position at your extreme stretch. Return to the starting position. Repeat, reversing directions.

Breathing

Breathing is normal and regulated.

Posture

Be sure to keep the knees locked (but not hyperextended) throughout the exercise. Do not shift your hips during the stretch or you may put excessive strain on the knees.

Remarks

This exercise should be done at a very slow, steady pace, holding each position a few seconds at the point of maximum stretch.

As you rotate your upper body, try to keep your head the same distance from the ground although you will probably find it possible to lower your body further in the forward position than in the side position. You may, at first, find the side and back stretches vary uncomfortably due to stiffness in the waist. Because of this initial stiffness, it is very important to warm up briefly as described above.

Concentration

Waist area, abdominals, lower back, legs and hips.

WAIST ROTATIONS

1

2

3

WAIST ROTATIONS

4

5

6

WAIST ROTATIONS (Variation)

Stance

    Feet together.

Description

    Warm up by slowly rotating in a circle at your own pace, then reverse direction. This loosens up the hips and lower back.

    Put your hands on your hips. Bend forward until chest is parallel to the ground. Your back is slightly arched and your head is looking straight forward. Keeping your legs locked and your lower body stationary, slowly roll your body to the right until your right side is parallel to the ground. Keep your upper body in line with your lower body to obtain the maximum stretch of your left waist muscles. Next roll your body backwards. Arch your back as if beginning a back bend and let your head fall backwards. This stretches the abdominal muscles and lower back.

    Continue rolling to the left side holding the position at your extreme stretch. Return to the starting position. Repeat, reversing directions.

Posture

    Keep the legs locked (but not hyperextended) throughout the exercise.

Breathing

    Normal and regulated breathing.

Remarks

    By standing with the feet together, the waist area will seem much tighter and the rotation will be more difficult. With continued work; however, a greater degree of flexibility will be obtained. This variation also enhances your sense of balance. Remember to keep your knees locked, but not hyperextended.

Concentration

    Waist area, abdominals, lower back, hips and legs.

WAIST ROTATIONS (Variation)

1

2

3

4

5

6

WAIST BEND

Stance

Beginner: Feet shoulder width apart. Intermediate: Feet spread apart approximately a foot wider than shoulder width. Advanced: Feet spread apart approximately a foot wider than shoulder width.

Description

Begin with your hands over your head, the left hand grasping the right wrist. Keeping your upper body over the lower body, slowly pull your body to the left side your right side is parallel to the ground. Do not arch your body pointing it towards the floor. Instead, your body and arms should be pointing straight out. Hold at the point of maximum stretch of the waist and lateral muscles. Return to the starting position and reverse the stretch, pulling your body to the right side and grasping the left wrist with right hand.

Posture

Make sure that your back is straight and that your head is directly between your hands when assuming the starting position.

Remarks

When returning to the original position, you may feel a strain in the muscles which have been stretched. This is a normal result of the stretching process. Be careful not to jerk your body upright but maintain a smooth, steady movement.

Concentration

All side muscles inclusive, lateral muscles, waist, hips and legs.

WAIST BEND

1

2

3

WAIST BEND

4

5

6

WAIST BEND - ARCH

Stance

Beginner: Feet shoulder width apart. Intermediate: Feet spread apart approximately a foot wider than shoulder width. Advanced: Feet spread apart approximately a foot wider than shoulder width.

Description

Begin with your hands over your head, your left hand grasping the right wrist. Keeping your upper body in a straight line over the lower body, slowly pull your body to the left side until your left side is parallel to the ground. After pointing straight out away from the body, continue bending your waist, arching to the floor and into your body. Your fingertips point to the ground and your arms are parallel to your leg. Return to the original position and reverse your direction to the right, grasping your left wrist with your right hand.

Remarks

This variation puts greater pressure on the sides of the waist, increasing the degree of stretch.

Concentration

All side muscles inclusive, lateral muscles, waist hips and legs.

WAIST BEND - ARCH

1

3

2

WAIST BEND - ARCH

4

5

6

WAIST BENDS ■ 45 DEGREE ANGLE

Stance
Beginner: Feet shoulder width apart. Intermediate: Feet spread apart approximately a foot wider than shoulder width. Advanced: Feet spread apart approximately a foot wider than shoulder width.

Description
Begin with your hands over your head, the left hand grasping the right wrist. Keeping your upper body in a straight line over the lower body, slowly pull your body to the left side until your left side is parallel to the ground. Do not arch your body pointing to the floor. Instead, your body and arms should be pointing straight out from the trunk. Hold at the point of maximum stretch of the waist and lateral muscles. Slowly rotate the body to a forty-five degree angle keeping your side parallel to the ground. Hold at the point of maximum stretch. Then rotate your upper body directly in front of you. Your chest is facing towards the right with your left side at right angles to your lower body. Hold at the point of maximum stretch.

Now rotate the body putting your right side at right angles to your lower body. At the same time, switch hands, your right hand is now grasping your left wrist. Rotate your body forty-five degrees until you have reached the point of maximum stretch over your right hip.

Return to the starting position. Repeat, rotating first to the right side.

Breathing
Normal, regulated breathing.

Remarks
Because the waist is twisted at different angles, this variation stretches muscles which are not affected by the normal waist-bend exercise.

Make sure you keep your head at the same level throughout the rotation. Do not bob your head. Your legs should remain locked throughout the entire exercise.

Concentration
All side muscles inclusive, lateral muscles, waist, hips and legs.

WAIST BENDS ■ 45 DEGREE ANGLE

1

2

3

WAIST BENDS - 45 DEGREE ANGLE

4

5

6

ARM CLASP WAIST TWIST

Stance

Square Horse

Description

Begin with the hands pressed together and extended directly in front of the body. Keeping the back straight and head erect, turn the entire upper body to the left side. Your chest and extended arms should be pointed to the left side. Hold at the point of maximum stretch. Return to the starting position and then reverse direction, twisting to the right side. Hold and return to the starting position.

Breathing

Inhale in the starting position. Exhale as you twist. When you have reached the point of maximum stretch, begin your normal regulated breathing. Inhale, then exhale as you twist back to the starting position.

Posture

Make sure that your heels are pushed out, your hips are tucked under, and your knees are projected over your toes. As you gain in flexibility, continue to lower your stance.

Remarks

Because the stance keeps your hips locked forward, this exercise concentrates solely on your waist. Be careful not to jerk your body suddenly when twisting from side to side. Maintain a slow, steady pace.

As you rotate to each side, you will notice that the knee on the opposite side has a tendency to turn in. Make sure you tense your thigh muscles to keep the knees pointed over the toes. This further strengthens the leg muscles.

Be sure to keep your hands pressed together, palm to palm throughout the entire exercise.

Concentration

Waist, lower back, hips, legs and abdominals.

ARM CLASP WAIST TWIST

1

2

3

ARM CLASP WAIST TWIST

4

5

6

WAIST BENDS - CHEST PRESS

Stance

Beginner: Shoulder width apart. Intermediate: Feet spread apart approximately a foot wider than shoulder width. Advanced: Feet spread apart approximately a foot wider than shoulder width.

Description

Begin with your legs straight (the knees are locked but not hyperextended), your back is straight, and your head is erect. Begin by turning left from the waist. When your body reaches a forty-five degree angle, press your chest forward. As you continue rotating, leading with your chest; your right hand reaches forward, your right palm is facing back and your left hand reaches back with left palm facing front. Imagine that you are stretching for something just out of reach. Hold at the point of maximum stretch. Slowly return to the starting position with your hands at your sides. Repeat on the other side.

Breathing

Inhale as you reach forward with the chest. Maintain normal regulated breathing at the point of maximum stretch. Inhale, then exhale as you return to starting position.

Posture

Make sure that your legs stay underneath the upper body and do not bend. Keep your hips locked forward to increase the stretch in the waist.

Remarks

Thrusting the chest forward and keeping the legs locked stretches the back muscles and the muscles of the upper legs as well as the waist muscles.

Concentration

Waist, lower back, hips, legs and hamstrings.

WAIST BENDS - CHEST PRESS

1

2

3

4

WAIST BENDS - CHEST PRESS

5

6

7

8

WAIST BEND - CHEST ROTATION

Stance

Beginner: Feet shoulder width apart. Intermediate: Feet spread apart approximately a foot wider than shoulder width. Advanced: Feet spread apart approximately a foot wider than shoulder width.

Description

Begin with your legs straight (knees locked but not hyperextended), back straight, head erect. Begin turning left from the waist. When your body reaches a forty-five degree angle, press your chest forward. Leading with the chest, begin rotating your body to the left. While your left hand reaches to the ceiling, reach with your right hand to your left heel. Hold at the point of maximum stretch, return to original position. Repeat reversing directions.

Remarks

By reaching toward the ground, you intensify the stretch in the waist as well as stretching the legs and hamstrings. It is vital to keep your legs straight. If you are unable to touch your heels and feel some strain, continue reaching slowly injhat direction without touching your heels. As your flexibility increases try to place your palm flat by your heel and stretch your body until your side is parallel to your legs. Greater flexibility will soon be attained.

Concentration

Waist, lower back, hips, abdominal area, legs and hamstrings.

WAIST BEND ■ CHEST ROTATION

1

2

3

HIP ROTATIONS

Stance

Feet together.

Description

Begin with the legs and back straight and your hands on your waist. Keeping your upper body directly over your lower body; begin rotating the hips forward, right, back, left and return to the starting position. Use a smooth, steady rolling motion. Rotate several times to the right; then reverse directions.

Breathing

Normal, regulated breathing.

Posture

Back straight, legs locked (but not hyperextended). Keep shoulders and feet stationary.

Remarks

This rotation is excellent for loosening the hips and working the waist. It is important to be warmed up before practicing this exercise.

Concentration

Waist and hips.

HIP ROTATIONS

1

2

3

4

PELVIC THRUST

Stance

Feet together.

Description

Start with your hands on your hips, legs straight, back erect. Tucking the buttocks under while thrusting the pelvis forward, hold while tightening the buttock muscles. Relax the muscles and return to the starting position. Then arch the lower back while keeping the upper back straight. Hold, tightening the buttock muscles which are now thrust out behind the body. Relax the muscles and return to the starting position.

Breathing

Normal, regulated breathing.

Posture

Body straight, legs straight, head erect.

Remarks

This exercise is excellent for loosening the hips and lower back while firming the buttocks.

Concentration

Hips, lower back, buttocks and lower abdominals.

PELVIC THRUST

1

2

3

4

HIP LIFTS

Stance
Feet together with the knees bent slightly.

Description
Begin with back straight and the hands on the waist. Lift the right hip, rolling onto the ball of the right foot. Return to starting position. Repeat on the left side. Alternate from side to side at a steady pace.

Breathing
Normal, regulated breathing.

Posture
The back is straight and the hips are tucked under the body.

Remarks
Because this exercise provides a concentrated workout for the waist area. You may develop a side ache during your first practice sessions. As you gain greater flexibility and control, try to bring your hip up as far as possible to increase the effect on the waist area.

Concentration
Hips, waist and feet.

HIP LIFTS

i

2

3

4

CROSS CHEST LIFTS

Stance

Feet are placed shoulder width apart.

Description

Begin with the back straight, the legs locked and the arms extended out with palms facing the floor. Lift the right knee aiming at the left shoulder. Keep your toes pointed. Slowly lower your leg to the starting position. Then lift the right knee towards the arm pit of the right arm. Return to the starting position. Repeat with left knee. Be sure to keep the toes pointed on the lifting leg.

Breathing

Inhale, then exhale as you lift your knee. Inhale as you return to the starting position.

Posture

Keep your back straight and hips locked forward throughout the exercise. The head is erect, looking forward.

Remarks

This exercise is intended to isolate one hip joint at a time—the hip joint on the side of the moving leg. For this reason, keep your shoulders and the hip joint on the opposing side stationary.

When lifting your leg across your chest, you are also strengthening the lower abdominal muscles as well as the muscles in the upper leg.

As you lift your leg towards the armpit, you are strengthening and firming your waist.

Be sure to begin practicing this exercise at a medium pace. Do not speed up the pace until you become more familiar with this movement.

Your stationary leg may wobble when you begin this exercise. Greater stability will come with practice.

Concentration

Hip, waist, lower abdominal muscles, buttocks, legs and lower back.

CROSS CHEST LIFTS

1

2

3

4

WAIST CRUNCH

Stance

Propped position on side.

Description

Lie on your left side, propping your upper body off the floor with your left arm. Place the right hand on floor in front of the body to aid in maintaining your balance. Pulling the right knee up, point the toe and pull to along the side of the left leg until the toe reaches the knee. The right knee should be pointed at the ceiling. Making sure the body stays upright, extend the leg straight out. The top of the foot should remain pointed towards the ceiling. As you slowly lower the leg to the starting position, allow the foot to rotate towards the front of your body. Repeat this on your right side.

Breathing

Inhale as you pull the leg up. Exhale as you extend the leg and lower it to the starting point.

Posture

Make sure the body stays propped up and stationary. You should feel a slight pressure in the waist area.

Remarks

This exercise concentrates on firming the waist area. Because your body is propped up to intensify the waist conditioning, you may feel cramping in this area at first. The conditioning will only be effective if the body is kept stationary and in a propped up position. Do not lower the body while extending the leg.

Variation

As you gain flexibility, try to bring your extended leg close to your head. As an aid, you may wish to grasp your ankle and gently pull the leg.

Concentration

Waist, hips, lower abdominals, buttocks and legs.

WAIST CRUNCH

1

2

3

WAIST CRUNCH

4

5

SIT UPS - AGAINST THE WALL

Starting Position

Sit upright on the floor with the knees bent, facing a wall. Press the balls of your feet into the wall, heels on the floor, as if pressing the gas pedal of a car. Keep your hands on your waist or place them on the stomach.

Description

Begin slowly lowering your body as far as possible. When you have reached the lowest point possible without touching the floor, pull the body back up to the starting position. Repeat.

Breathing

Inhale as you lower your body. Exhale as you return to a sitting position.

Remarks

This sit-up variation works both the upper and lower abdominal regions. By keeping a steady pressure on your legs as you raise and lower the body, you will strengthen the lower abdominals. The upper abdominals are strengthened in controlling the movement of the upper body.

As your muscles become stronger, you will be able to lower your back until it is parallel to, but not touching, the ground. You may wish to slightly tip the head to increase the pressure on the abdominals and the lower back at an advanced state of this exercise.

Keep your knees together.

Posture

Keep your back straight and head in line with the body throughout the exercise. Remember to relax your shoulders and upper body.

Concentration

Lower and upper abdominals, legs, ankles, feet and lower back.

SIT UPS ■ AGAINST THE WALL

1

2

3

4

TWISTED SIT-UP

Starting Position

Sit upright on the floor with the knees bent, facing a wall. Press the balls of your feet into the wall with the heels on the floor, as if pressing the gas pedal of a car. The arms are extended in front of the body with the palms together.

Description

Swing the right arm directly behind your body, turning your upper to the right. Slowly lower the body down as far as possible, keeping your arms parallel to the floor. Do not let the body touch the floor. As you pull your body up, turn it to the front as you return to the starting position. Maintain steady pressure on your legs. Repeat on the left side.

Breathing

Inhale as you lower the body. Exhale as you sit up.

Posture

Turn the waist as far as possible to each side. Your legs remain directly in front of you throughout the entire exercise.

Remarks

Because you are twisting the waist during the sit-up, you may feel cramping in your side or abdominal muscles. Keep your legs together and back as straight as possible throughout the exercise. Eventually, you should be able to lower your side until it is parallel to the floor without touching it.

Pay attention to your breathing pattern.

Concentration

Lower and upper abdominals, waist, lower back, legs, ankles and feet.

TWISTED SIT-UP

1

2

3

4

SIT UP ABDOMINALS ONLY

Starting Position

Sit on the floor, knees slightly bent, feet flat on the floor and arms held close to the waist.

Description

Slowly lower the body down as far as possible keeping your back straight. Return to the starting position.

Breathing

Inhale while lowering the body and exhale while returning to the starting position.

Posture

Keep your head and back in a straight line. When you have lowered your body to the floor, you should be looking up at the ceiling.

Remarks

Keep your upper body, particularly the shoulders, as relaxed as possible. Be sure your feet remain flat on the floor without pushing into the ground. Eventually, you should be able to lower your body until it is almost parallel to the floor with only the buttocks touching the floor.

This exercise should be performed at a moderate pace without jerking your body and causing undue stress.

Do not cheat by using the arms or upper portion of your body to pull yourself up.

Concentration

Upper and lower abdominals.

SIT UP ABDOMINALS ONLY

1

2

3

SIT UP ABDOMINALS ONLY

4

5

6

LOWER BODY (LEG) EXERCISES

SIDE LEG LIFTS

Starting Position

Lie on your left side with your body in a straight line. Your left arm reaches over your body to rest on the right side of your waist. Your right hand rests on the floor in front of your body and helps support your upper body slightly off the floor. Point the toes of both legs.

Description

Lift your right leg up as high as possible. Hold at the point of maximum stretch and then slowly lower the leg to its original position. Repeat this series with toes flexed. Then repeat the entire exercise on your right side.

Breathing

Inhale, then exhale, while lifting the leg. Inhale while lowering the leg.

Posture

Hold the upper body as far off the gound as possible. Do not allow the leg to rotate towards the ceiling as you raise it. Keep your body in a straight line.

Remarks

Practice this exercise at a moderate pace. You should feel some tension in the waist area. By alternating the pointed and flexed position of the toes, you will exercise different leg and foot muscles.

Concentration

Waist, hips and legs.

SIDE LEG LIFTS

1

2

3

LEG LIFT - BOTH LEGS

Starting Position

Lie on your left side with the body in a straight line. Your left arm reaches over your body to rest on the right side of your waist. Your right hand rests on the floor in front of your body and hold your upper body slightly off the floor. Point the toes of both legs.

Description

Lift both legs from the floor. Hold. Slowly lift the right leg as high as possible, while maintaining the position of the left leg. Slowly lower the leg to the original position. Repeat the exercise with the toes flexed. Then repeat the entire series on the right side.

Remarks

By holding the stationary leg slightly off the ground, you strengthen the muscles in that leg as well. Make sure the stationary leg does not drop as you are lifting and lowering the top leg.

Concentration

1   2

LEG LIFT ■ BOTH LEGS

3

4

5

LEG LIFT - SCISSORS

Starting Position

Lie on your left side with the body in a straight line. Your left arm reaches over your body to rest on the right side of your waist. Your right hand rests on the floor in front of your body and holds your upper body slightly off the floor. Point the toes of both legs.

Description

Lift both legs at least six inches off the ground with the toes pointed. Slowly swing the left leg back with the right leg forward. Hold at the point of maximum stretch, then reverse the swing with the right leg back and the left leg forward. Continue alternating your legs in a scissors motion. Return to the original position. Repeat on your right side.

Remarks

Keep your upper body as stationary as possible. Only your legs should move. Be sure to control your movements. Swing slowly, rather than with jerky, unstable motions. Do not lower your legs. Rather, continue to raise them as you proceed with the exercise.

Concentration

Waist, abdominals, hips and legs.

LEG LIFT • SCISSORS

1

2

3

LEG LIFT - SCISSORS

4

5

6

LEG LIFT - INNER THIGH

Starting Position

Lie on your left side with your body in a straight line. Your left arm reaches over your body to rest on the right side of your waist. Your right hand rests on the floor in front of your body and helps to support your upper body slightly off the floor. Point the toes of both legs.

Description

Flex the right foot and lift the right leg as far as possible. The leg should be, at least, at a right angle to the left leg. Slowly lower the leg towards the floor and hold it parallel to the floor. Slowly raise the leg and lower it to the starting position. Repeat on the right side.

Breathing.

Inhale and exhale as you lift the leg. Inhale as you lower the leg to the floor. Exhale as you lift the leg to the right angle position. Inhale as you return the leg to the starting position.

Remarks

Make sure the foot remains flexed and body propped up as high as possible throughout the entire exercise.

Variations

You can vary this exercise as follows:
1. After you have lowered the leg in front of you, slowly lift the leg to the right angle position. Lower the leg in front of you again and repeat the raising and lowering movement.
2. After you have lowered the leg in front of you, swing the leg back towards the extended left leg keeping it the same distance above the floor. Repeat the series of movements.

By making your legs work against gravity, these variations are particularly good for strengthening the inner and outer thigh muscles.

Concentration

Waist, abdominals, inner and outer thigh and hips.

LEG LIFT - INNER THIGH

1

2

3

LEG LIFT - INNER THIGH

4

5

6

LEGS - MOONWALKING

Starting Position

Lie on your back with your hands on your stomach, legs together and feet flexed.

Description

Slowly raise both legs to a right angle position. Keeping the legs straight and using dynamic tension, bend the right knee as if a heavy weight were resting on your foot. Then press the leg up straight and repeat with the left leg.

Breathing

Inhale when lowering the 1军. Exhale when pressing the leg up.

Posture

Keep your back flat on the floor. Make sure you keep the hips on the ground.

Remarks

Avoid straining your lower back. As you become more familiar with the use of dynamic tension in this position, begin to pump your legs using a smooth, steady motion. Keep them at a right angle to the body while maneuvering the legs.

Concentration

Lower back, abdomen, legs and ankles.

LEGS - MOONWALKING

1

2

3

LEGS • MOONWALKING

4

5

CROSS LEG LIFT

Starting Position
The back is straight, the right leg extended and the left leg crossed over right with the left foot flat on the floor by left knee. Your hands are on your waist.

Description
Begin lifting the right leg as high as possible working against the resistance of the crossed left leg. Alternate pointing and flexing the right foot. Repeat with the left leg extended and the left leg crossed.

Breathing
Normal, regulated breathing.

Posture
Your back should remain straight with the head erect.

Remarks
Keep the foot of the crossed over leg flat on the floor. Press it into the floor, if necessary, to resist the lifting leg.

Do not lean back or forward to help raise the leg. Isolate the effort in the thigh muscles.

Concentration
Lower abdominals, thighs, calves, ankles and feet.

CROSS LEG LIFT

1

2

3

4

LEG SQUAT

Starting Position

The feet are together, arms extended straight overhead and your fingertips are pointing to the ceiling.

Description

Bend the knees until you are lowered into a half-knee bend position, with the thighs parallel to the floor. Bending at the waist, lower the chest until it is parallel to the thighs. Be sure not to rest your chest on your thighs. The arms are extended straight out in front of you. Pull the body back to the bent-knee position. Repeat, then straighten the legs until you have returned to the original starting position.

Breathing

Normal, regulated breathing.

Posture

Keep the back as straight as possible with the knees bent. Keep the head in alignment with the upper body at all times.

Remarks

In the squatting position, press your legs together. Keep your buttocks tucked under your body. Do not squat down so that your buttocks are resting on your heels. When bending forward, concentrate on keeping your back as flat as possible. When your hands are extended out, reach with your fingertips as if trying to grab something.

Concentration

Lower back, abdominals, upper thigh and ankles.

LEG SQUAT

1

2

3

4

LEG LIFTS

Starting Position

Lie flat on your back, hands on your stomach. Your legs are together with the toes pointed out.

Description

Lift both legs six inches off the ground. Hold that position. Separate the legs as far as possible. Hold, then return your legs together without lowering them. Raise your legs six more inches, separate them and bring the legs together again. Continue raising and separating the legs until they are at right angles to the floor. Repeat the same pattern as you bring them back to the floor.

Breathing

Exhale during maximum exertion. Inhale at all other times.

Posture

Keep the back flat on the ground pressing the lower back into the floor. Your hands remain on the stomach.

Remarks

Maintain a steady pace throughout the exercise so as not to overly strain the lower abdominal region. Since the hands remain on your stomach rather than pressing on the floor, your abdominal muscles will need to work harder and you may feel some strain.

Variations

You may wish to try the following variations as you raise and lower your legs.
1. Flex your toes as you separate and return your legs.
2. Lift your legs six inches from the ground. Separate your legs, then lift them, separate in several stages until they are at right angles to the floor. Bring your legs together, then slowly lower to the floor.
3. Lift your legs six incheg, then separate your legs. Lift your legs while separated, six inches, then lower six inches. Repeat several times. Then, bring your legs together and lower them to the ground.

Concentration

Lower abdominals, lower back, hips and legs.

LEG LIFTS

1

2

3

LEG LIFTS

4

5

6

LEG LIFTS

8

9

10

SCISSOR LEG LIFTS

Starting Position

Lie flat on your back with your hands on your stomach. Keep your legs together with the toes pointed.

Description

Slowly lift the legs until they are at right angles to the floor. Lower the right leg until it is parallel to the ground without touching it. Slowly alternate the legs in a scissoring motion. After repeating this several times, bring both legs to a right angle position and lower them to the floor together.

Breathing

Normal, regulated breathing.

Posture

Keep the back flat on the ground. Press your lower back into the floor. The hands should remain on your stomach.

Remarks

Maintain a steady pace throughout the exercise and avoid short, jerky motions. Concentrate on regulating your breathing to facilitate this exercise.

You may feel an uncomfortable strain in the lower abdomen. Do not overdo this exercise or overly strain yourself. Keep the upper portion of your body relaxed.

Concentration

Lower abdomen, legs, lower back and hips.

SCISSOR LEG LIFTS

1

2

3

SIDE-TO-SIDE LEG LIFTS

Starting Position

Lie flat on your back with the legs together and the toes pointed. Your arms are stretched out sideways with the palms on the floor.

Description

Lift your right knee to your chest keeping the toes pointed. Twist your right knee across your body to the left arm, then extend your leg with the toes pointed towards the fingertips of the left hand. Keep your shoulders flat on the ground. Slowly lift the extended leg straight up and over to the right extending it straight out towards the fingertips of the right hand. The leg should not touch the ground. Swing the leg back to the extended left leg and lower it to the ground.

Breathing

Inhale as you lift the knee up. Exhale as you twist the right knee across the body. Inhale, then exhale as you swing the leg over your body and return it to the left leg.

Posture

Keep your back as flat as possible pressing the lower portion of your back into the ground. Your arms are extended throughout the exercise. One leg is always extended on the floor.

Remarks

Press your palms into the floor, if necessary, to keep your shoulders flat.

As you achieve greater flexibility try to keep the distance between your leg and your upper body as short as possible.

Proceed at a moderate pace. Because of the twisting movement in this exercise you do not want to jerk the lower back.

Concentration

Shoulders, waist, lower abdominals, hips, legs, ankles and the lower back.

SIDE-TO-SIDE LEG LIFTS

1

2

3

SIDE-TO-SIDE LEG LIFTS

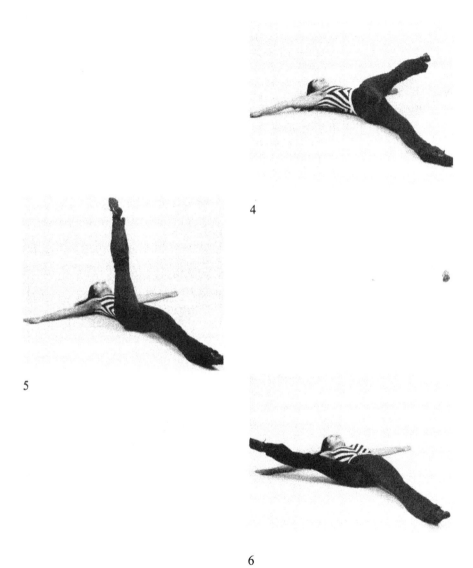

4

5

6

SIDE-TO-SIDE LEG LIFTS - LEGS EXTENTED

Starting Position

Lie flat on your back, legs together and toes pointed. Your arms are stretched out sideways, palms on the floor.

Description

Raise both legs to a right angle position. Keeping your legs pinched together, lower your legs slowly to the right side until they are parallel to the floor. Return to the right angle position. Repeat, lowering them to the left side. Return to the right angle position and then lower both legs to the floor very slowly.

Breathing

Exhale while lowering your legs to the floor. Inhale when lifting the legs to the right angle position. Inhale, then exhale and return to the right angle position.

a
Posture

Keep your shoulders, arms and back flat on the floor throughout the exercise.

Remarks

Be sure to keep your legs pinched firmly together. Control your motion as you lower your legs so there are no fast, jerky motions.
The legs should not touch the floor when lowered to the sides.
Be careful not to put excessive strain on the lower back.

Concentration

Lower back, waist, upper and lower abdominals and the legs.

SIDE-TO-SIDE LEG LIFTS - LEGS EXTENTED

1

2

3

4

SIDE-TO-SIDE LEG LIFTS - LEGS EXTENTED

5

6

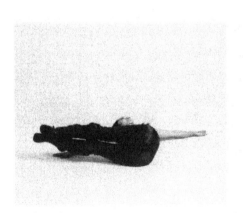

7

8

V-UPS

Starting Position

Sit erect on the floor, legs together, knees tucked in to the chest and the toes pointed. The arms are braced slightly behind the buttocks.

Description

Keeping the back straight, slowly extend the legs straight up. Toes remain pointed and the legs pressed together. Hold the legs as high and as tight into the body as possible without losing your balance. Then slowly lower the legs and tuck them into the body. Repeat.

Breathing

Inhale in the starting position. Exhale as you extend your legs. Inhale again as you tuck the legs into your body.

Posture

Keep your back straight. Body should hold a "V" shape in a tucked and extended position. The head remains in line with the body looking forward.

Remarks

Use the arms, only as a brace, don't rest your weight on them. At the advanced level, the "V"-ups should be done without the use of the arms.

Remember to keep the legs together.

The extending and tucking motion are all done at a moderate pace which is controlled, slow and steady. This enhances the toning effect on the abdominals.

If you have a problem keeping the back straight, shift your focus point by tilting the head slightly to look at the area where the wall and ceiling meet. This forces your chest up and keeps the lower back from sagging.

Vary this exercise by pointing and then flexing your toes.

Concentration

Upper and lower abdominals, lower back, hips and legs.

V-UPS

1

2

3

4

SEPARATED V-UPS

Starting Position

Starting from the previous V-up position and keeping the back straight, slowly extend the legs straight up. The toes remain pointed and the legs are pressed together. Hold the legs as high as possible without losing your balance. Slowly separate the legs, controlling the movement, until they are as far apart as possible. Slowly return the legs together keeping them extended straight out in front of the body. Bend your knees to tuck your legs into your body. Repeat.

Posture

Keep your back straight, the body should hold a "V" shape in the tucked and extended position. The head remains in line with the body looking forward. Be sure to keep your back straight.

Breathing

Inhale in the starting position. Exhale as you extend your legs and separate them. Inhale as you bring your legs together and return them to the tucked position.

Remarks

By separating the legs you intensify the tension on the lower abdominal region. At the same time, you stretch the inner thigh muscles. After you have separated the legs and brought them back together, continue the motion of separating and returning the legs together.

Concentration

Upper and lower abdominals, lower back, hips and legs.

SEPARATED V-UPS

i

2

3

4

WAIST - SITTING TWISTS

Starting Position

Sit erect on the floor, legs together, knees tucked into the chest, and the toes pointed. The arms are braced slightly behind the body.

Description

With the back straight, twist the waist to lower the knees to the left side. The legs should be pinched together and held parallel to the floor. Hold at the point of maximum stretch. Slowly rotate the knees over to the right side. Hold at the point of maximum stretch. Repeat the sequence.

Breathing

Inhale while lowering your knees. Exhale while shifting positions.

Posture

Keep the head in line with the body and the back straight. The shoulders should be straight and facing forward.

Remarks

Twist at the waist and lower the knees but hold the upper body erect and keep as much of the buttocks and hips on the ground as possible. You should feel tension in your waist—this indicates that you are practicing the exercise correctly. To intensify the effect, you may twist the shoulders slightly in the opposite direction to the knees.

This exercise also provides a gentle stretch of the lower back, avoid any jerky motions.

Variation

You can vary this exercise by extending the legs out straight after lowering them to each side. Be sure to keep the legs together.

Concentration

Lower back, abdomen, waist and buttocks.

WAIST - SITTING TWISTS

1

2

3

4

LEGS - TOE RAISES

Starting Position

Put the feet together, the head is erect looking forward, and the back is straight. Put your hands on your hips.

Description

Raise your body up onto the balls of your feet. Your knees are locked but not hyperextended. After you have come up on the balls of your feet, tighten your buttocks and legs. Hold them and then slowly lower your feet back to the starting position.

From this position, push your toes out until the feet are in a V-shape. Repeat, coming up onto the balls of your feet. Hold, then lower your body. Repeat. Bring the toes back to the starting position.

From this position, push your heels out until the feet are pigeon-toed. Come up onto the balls of your feet. Hold. Then lower your body and repeat. From this position, keep the heels stationary and move the toes out. Your feet are now approximately a shoulder width apart. Come up on the balls of your feet. Hold then lower your body. Repeat.

From this position, come up onto the balls of your feet. Keeping the left foot up, lower your right heel to the ground. Raise the right heel up and lower the left heel to the ground. Repeat, alternating legs.

Breathing

Normal, regulated breathing.

Posture

Your back should remain straight with the head erect, and looking forward. Keep your hips tucked under your body.

Remarks

Make sure your legs are warmed up before practicing this exercise. If you have had shin splints or any other leg injuries, or if you are prone to

LEGS - TOE RAISES

leg cramps, be very careful when you are practicing this exercise.

The raising and lowering motions should be done slowly. Don't jar or strain your body or injure your heels by dropping your heels hard as you lower your body.

When you alternate raising your left and right foot, be sure to raise the corresponding hip.

Concentration

Buttocks, hips, thighs, calves, shins, ankles, toes and arches.

1

2

LEGS - TOE RAISES

3

4

5

6

LEGS - TOE RAISES

7

8

9

STRETCHING EXERCISES

ARM STRETCHES

Starting Position

Stand erect with the back straight and the feet shoulder width apart. The arms are extended in front of the body with the palms pressed together.

Description

Cross your right hand over your left hand with the palms facing out. Rotate the hands down until the palms face each other. Interlock the fingers. Turn the locked hands in towards your body and stop when your hands are clasped in front of your chest. From this position, pull the hands down exerting tension on the wrists. Hold at the point of maximum stretch. Relax the wrists and press the hands straight forward. With the elbows remaining locked, flex the wrists towards and away from your body. Pull the hands back towards your body until they are again clasped in front of your chest. Return to the starting position. Cross your left hand over your right hand and repeat the exercise.

Breathing

Normal, regulated breathing.

Posture

Keep your back straight throughout the exercise. Your shoulders should be relaxed at all times.

Remarks

When beginning this exercise, be careful not to overstrain the wrists. If your wrists are very tight you may not be able to flex them completely. This flexibility will come with repeated work.

If the arms cannot be fully extended, stretch them out to their maximum point of stretch.

Concentration

Shoulders, biceps, triceps, forearms, wrists and fingers.

ARM STRETCHES

1

2

3

ARM STRETCHES

4

5

6

BACK OF WRISTS STRETCH

Starting Position

The feet are shoulder width apart, the back is straight and the head is erect. The arms are in front of your chest, the hands are back to back and the fingers are pointed up.

Description

Let the hands sink downwards towards your stomach without separating the hands and keeping them close into the body. Hold them at the point of maximum stretch. From that position, turn your hands over so the fingers are now pointing down. Raise the wrists keeping the hands together. The elbows are now pushing down. Return to the starting position.

Press the hands out in front of you. Hold at the point of maximum stretch. Repeat.

Breathing

Normal, regulated breathing.

Posture

The back should remain straight and the shoulders must be relaxed.

Remarks

As your wrists achieve greater flexibility, apply more pressure and raise and lower your wrists to more extreme positions. Try to keep your arms relaxed when pressing and avoid tightening up any part of the upper body.

Concentration

Shoulders, biceps, triceps, forearms, wrists and fingers.

BACK OF WRISTS STRETCH

1

2

3

4

SHOULDER STRETCH -BEHIND THE BACK

Starting Position

Stand erect with the right arm grabbing the left arm above the elbow behind the back. The palm of the right hand is facing away from the back.

Description

Your right arm pulls the left arm across the back towards the right side of the body. Hold at the point of maximum stretch. Relax the arms as the right arm releases the left. Repeat with the left arm grabbing and pulling the right.

Breathing

Normal, regulated breathing.

Posture

Back straight, head erect.

Remarks

When pulling on the extended arm, do not twist the body at the waist.
The shoulder of the grabbing arm should remain facing forward. Only the shoulder being stretched moves slightly towards the rear.
Do not arch the back.

Concentration

Shoulders, biceps and pectorals.

SHOULDER STRETCH - BEHIND THE BACK

1

2

3

4

LEG STRETCH - STANDING

Starting Position

Feet together, back straight and arms at your side.

Description

Bending at your waist and keeping the legs straight, reach towards your feet with your fingertips. The top of your head should be in alignment with your toes. Try to make your chest parallel to your legs as if your body was being folded at your waist. Twisting at the waist but keeping your body bent and stretched, slowly reach with your fingertips towards the right heel. Then bring your fingertips around and reach towards the left heel. Repeat this swinging motion. Return your fingertips to your toes. Bend your knees and slowly raise your body. Keeping your legs together, press down on the upper thigh area with the palms of your hands. Hold and then repeat the exercise. Between each full stretch, return to the bent leg pushing position.

Breathing

Inhale in the starting position, exhale as you reach down. Maintain normal, regulated breathing or slightly slower breathing then normal throughout each full stretch.

Posture

It is essential to keep the backs of the legs straight with knees locked but not hyperextended. The feet are placed together. When the knees are bent, be certain that they are pressed together.

Remarks

During the stretching exercise, hold the upper body as closely as possible to the legs. For maximum stretch, keep the head down. Slow, regulated breathing will help you keep your muscles relaxed. Be sure not to overstrain your body. Flexibility is acquired gradually. When swinging

LEG STRETCH - STANDING

your hands from side to side, be careful not to raise your body. Your upper body should remain as close to your legs as possible. In the bent position, make sure your back is straight and your buttocks tucked under your body. Your hand should be pushing on the upper thigh only, not on or near the knee.

Variations

You can vary this exercise as follows:

In the downward stretch position, try reaching with your palms to the floor with the backs of the hands and the wrists, with the arms folded and held at the elbows, and by grabbing the ankles and pulling your upper body to your legs.

Concentration

Lower back, backs of legs, hamstrings and the front of the thighs.

1

2

LEG STRETCH ■ STANDING

3

4

5

6

LEG STRETCH - STANDING

Variation 1

2

3

4

LEGS SEPARATED STRETCH

Starting Position

Stand erect with the back straight and the legs separated approximately one foot wider than your shoulder width. Your hands rest at your sides.

Description

Slowly reach between your legs to the floor until you reach the point of maximum stretch. Grab your ankles and pull your head towards the floor. The head should point towards the floor. Relax by bringing the body up slightly.

Still holding your ankles pull your head in between your legs towards your back. Relax and return to your original position.

Breathing

Normal, regulated breathing.

Posture

Your knees should be locked but not hyperextended. Keep your feet flat on the floor.

Remarks

When stretching the head to the floor, flatten out the lower back as much as possible. Be sure to keep the head in alignment with the body. If you are unable to reach the ankles, grab the back of the calves.

When stretching between your legs, keep your back as straight as possible. Your upper body should be either in line with the legs or reaching behind the line of the legs.

Concentration

Lower back, back of legs, hamstrings and hips.

LEGS SEPARATED STRETCH

1

2

3

HURDLE STRETCH - FRONT

Starting Position

Sit on the ground with back straight, with right leg extended and the left leg tucked so your left foot is next to the right knee.

Description

Reach forward to the right foot. Grab the ankle or heel and pull the upper body flat to the leg. The head should look towards the toes. Hold at the point of maximum stretch. Bring the body halfway up. Twist the body to the left. Grab the right foot with the left hand and rest your right hand on the left knee. Pull your right side to your right leg and hold at the point of maximum stretch. Return to the starting position. Repeat on the other side.

Breathing

Normal, regulated breathing.

Posture

Make sure the extended leg is straight and locked flat to the floor with the toes pointing up throughout the entire exercise.

Try to press the knee of the bent leg as flat as possible to the floor.

Remarks

When stretching forward, your chin and chest should reach towards your toes. Don't arch your back to drop your head to your knee as this prevents the lower back from stretching. Stretch until your stomach is parallel to your thigh, your chest to your knee, and your chin to your shin.

When stretching sideways, try to turn your body as far under the upper arm as possible in order to bring your rib cage as close to your leg.

If you are not flexible enough to grab your heel, you may grab your toe, ankle or hold onto a towel or belt wrapped around your foot.

As you gain flexibility, try to keep your body as relaxed as possible as you change from the front to the side stretch position. When shifting, continue to hold your right ankle with your left hand while reaching for your left knee with your right hand.

Concentration

Lower back, abdominals, hips, hamstrings and the back of the legs.

HURDLE STRETCH - FRONT

1

2

3

HURDLE STRETCH • FRONT

4

5

6

HURDLE STRETCH - BACK

Starting Position

Sitting on the floor with the right leg extended, the left leg is tucked behind the body in a hurdler's position.

Description

Reach forward over the extended leg, grabbing the heel. Stretch with the chin and chest looking at the toes. Hold at the point of maximum stretch. Again, reach with the chin and chest, this time to the floor. With the body still remaining low, stretch over the bent leg. Again, reach with the chin and chest. Try to put your chin on your knee. Hold at the point of maximum stretch. Reverse your direction, first stretching between your legs then over the extended leg. Repeat on the other side.

Breathing

Normal, regulated breathing.

Posture

Make sure the extended leg is locked flat to the floor and the foot is flexed. Keep the leg tucked behind the body flat on the floor.

Remarks

To increase the degree of stretch, flex the foot on the tucked leg. If you do not have the necessary flexibility to assume this position, you may turn the foot on its instep.

The tucked leg should at least be placed at a right angle to the body. To further increase the stretch, move the tucked leg beyond a right angle degree. When stretching over the back knee, try to flatten the back as much as possible. Avoid hunching the back.

Variation

You can vary this exercise by twisting the body sideways and then stretching over your forward leg and between the legs. Try to bring your ribcage as close to your leg and the floor as possible.

Concentration

Lower back, hamstrings, back of legs, hips and the waist.

HURDLE STRETCH - BACK

 1

 2

 3

 4

HURDLE STRETCH - BACK

5

6

7

8

LEGS EXTENDED - SITTING STRETCH

Starting Position

Sit on the floor with the legs extended straight out. The knees are locked and feet flexed.

Description

Reach forward, grabbing your heels and pull your body flat. Stretch forward with the chin and the chest looking at the toes. Press your stomach to your thighs with your chest to your knees and your chin to your shin. Release your heels, bring your body halfway up and grab your toes. Slowly pull your heels off the floor. Look at the ceiling and arch the lower back. Slowly lower the heels and repeat.

Breathing

Normal, regulated breathing.

Posture

The legs should remain locked and the toes flexed throughout the entire exercise.

Remarks

After you have grabbed your heels (or ankles, if you do not yet have sufficient flexibility, pull on your ankles as you lower your upper body. You will feel tension in your hamstrings and behind the knees. As you gain in flexibility, increase the amount of pull on your ankles to intensify the stretch. When you grab the toes to raise the heels, keep your elbows bent. By keeping the elbows bent, you will have more leverage for raising the heels. This exercise stretches the area behind the knees and the hamstrings. You may feel a great deal of tension at first, so maintain a slow, steady pull.

You may not be able to raise the heels at first. However, as you continue to pull your toes in this stretch, your heels will eventually rise. You may wish to pull on your shoe laces or socks to try to raise the heels.

Variation

You may vary this exercise as follows:
1. After you have pulled up the heels and returned them to the floor, retain your hold on the toes. Pull them towards you while slowly lowering

LEGS EXTENDED - SITTING STRETCH

your body. Repeat by pulling the heels off the ground.

    2. Separate your legs to shoulder width or one foot wider than shoulder width. Reaching between your legs, grab the inside of your feet at the instep. Pull your body forward, reaching with the chin and chest. Try to pull your head between your feet.

Concentration

1

2

LEGS EXTENDED - SITTING STRETCH

3

4

5

LEGS EXTENDED • SITTING STRETCH

6

7

8

HALF LOTUS STRETCH

Starting Position

    Sit flat on the floor with the head erect and the right leg crossed over the left.

Description

    Twist to the left, keeping your head in alignment with the body. Your left hand reaches behind your back and rests flat on the ground as close to your buttocks as possible. The right hand reaches to the left knee. Twist as far as possible and hold at the point of maximum stretch. Repeat in the reverse direction with the left leg crossed over the right.

Breathing

    Inhale as you twist, holding the air low in your diaphragm. Exhale slowly as you face forward.

Posture

    The back should remain straight and head in alignment with the body. Keep your buttocks flat on the floor.

Remarks

    The supporting hand behind the back must remain as close to the body as possible to keep the back in alignment. Use the hand resting on knee to help twist the body.

Variation

    You can vary this exercise as follows:
Inhale as you twist and hold to the maximum point of stretch. Then, as you exhale, increase the twist before returning to the front.

Concentration

    Lower back, hips, abdominals and shoulders.

HALF LOTUS STRETCH

1

2

3

4

PANCAKE STRETCH

Starting Position

Sit on the floor with the back straight and the legs tucked in, the soles of the feet are together. Place your hands on your ankles.

Description

Pull your feet as close to your crotch as possible. Grasping your ankles, use your elbows to push down on your knees. Keep your back—especially the lower back—as straight as possible. Hold at the point of maximum stretch. Relax the pressure of your elbows to release the tension on your legs. Begin pushing down with your elbows a second time. This time, reach forward with the chin and the chest. Hold at the point of maximum stretch. Bring your upper body back to the starting position and relax your elbows.

Extend your legs halfway out, keeping the soles of the feet together. Repeat the above series. Return to an upright position.

From this position, reverse your direction by pulling the legs back halfway and repeating the exercise. Finally return to the starting position with feet tucked tightly to the crotch.

Breathing

Inhale in the sitting position. Exhale while pressing the legs down and while leaning forward. Maintain normal, regulated breathing while holding the maximum point of stretch and during transition moves.

Posture

In the sitting position, the back should remain straight, the head in alignment with the body and the shoulders relaxed. When bending forward, keep the back straight.

Remarks

Try to relax the legs as much as possible. Use the leverage of the elbows to stretch the hips and groin areas.

When reaching forward, reach with the chin and chest rather than

PANCAKE STRETCH

merely dropping your head to your toes. This increases the stretch on the inner thigh areas.

Make sure the soles of the feet remain together throughout the exercise. You may wish to practice this exercise on a rug or towel to protect the ankle bones from becoming bruised.

Concentration

Hips, inner thigh, ankles and back.

1

2

PANCAKE STRETCH

3

4

5

6

TUCKED HURDLE STRETCH

Starting Position

Sit erect with left leg bent and tucked back in a hurdler's position at right angles to the body. Flex the left foot. The right leg is also bent in with foot parallel to the left knee. The arms are extended shoulder height to your sides.

Description

Twist your upper body at the waist as far as possible to the right side. Reach with the chin and chest to the floor. Hold at the point of maximum stretch and return to the starting position. Now twist your body as far as possible to the left side and reach with the chin and chest to your left knee. Hold at the point of maximum stretch and return to the starting position, repeat, switching your leg position.

Breathing

Inhale in the sitting position. Exhale as you twist to lower the body.

Posture

Keep your back straight, head erect and the shoulders relaxed in the sitting position. When reaching to the sides, keep your back as flat as possible.

Remarks

Make sure your body is warmed up before practicing this stretch. To get the maximum stretch, avoid arching the back. You will find that it is easier to twist the body away from the bent legs, the twist over the knees will put stress on the waist, hips and back. Increased flexibility will be attained in time and with continued practice.

To increase the stretch on the hip of the rear leg, flex the rear foot.

Concentration

Waist, abdominals, lower back and hips.

TUCKED HURDLE STRETCH

1

2

3

4

CROSSED KNEES STRETCH

Starting Position

The back is straight, head erect and facing forward. Bending the left leg, bring your left foot to the right hip. Bending your right leg, bring it over the left until your right knee is almost directly on top of your left knee and your right foot is close to your left hip.

Description

Grab your instep or ankles and pull them in towards your body. Twisting at the waist, reach to the right side. Hold at the point of maximum stretch. Return to the starting position. Keeping your back straight, twist to the left and lower your body to the left side. Return to the starting position. Repeat, switching leg positions.

Breathing

Inhale while sitting. Exhale while lowering the body.

Posture

Keep your back straight while sitting and as flat as possible while lowering the body.

Remarks

Since you will experience more tension when twisting your body towards the side of the under leg, you will want to work more on stretching in this direction.

Keep your feet flat and the buttocks and knees down on the ground throughout the exercise.

Concentration

Waist, lower back and hips.

CROSSED KNEES STRETCH

1

2

3

4

SPREAD LEG STRETCH

Starting Position

The back is straight and the head erect looking forward. The legs are spread out as far as possible. The feet are flexed.

Description

Raise your arms overhead and grab the right wrist with your left hand. Keeping your chest facing forward, slowly lower your body to the left side. At the same time, pull on the right wrist to stretch your right side. Continue lowering your body until your ribcage is flat on your legs. Hold at the point of maximum stretch. Slowly pull your body up to the sitting position. Reverse directions, grabbing the left wrist with your right hand. Hold at the point of maximum stretch. Return to the starting position. Let go of your wrist. Twist over your left leg reaching with your chin and chest. Grabbing your foot, pull your body forward. Hold, looking at your toes. Rotate between your legs, with the arms extended in front of you, reaching with your chin and chest. Rotate to your right leg. Grabbing your foot, pull your body forward. Repeat in the other direction. Raise your upper body straight up.

Finally, lower your body flat in front of you, reaching with your chin and chest to the floor. The arms are extended towards the feet. Return to the starting position.

Breathing

Inhale when sitting. Exhale as you lower yourself to the sides. Normal, regulated breathing when rotating positions.

Posture

When you pull your body from side to side, keep your chest forward, back straight, and head in alignment with the body.

When you pull your body over the extended legs, keep your back as straight as possible with the head facing forward.

Remarks

This exercise can be done with the feet flexed or pointed. You will increase the stretch with the feet flexed but you may wish to alternate positions as you repeat the exercise.

Whether pulling your body from side to side over the extended legs, pull out, as well as in towards the leg.

Make sure your legs are straight, pressed into the floor and separated as far as possible throughout the entire exercise.

SPREAD LEG STRETCH

Variations

You can vary the exercise as follows:

1. After pulling your body from side to side, instead of returning to the central upright position, turn at your waist so that your chest is facing one of your extended legs. Grab your heels and begin pulling yourself over your leg.

2. When you stretch your body forward between your legs, separate the exercise into the following stages: reach forward with your head; hold, then reach forward with your chin; hold, then reach forward with your chest; hold, then reach forward with your stomach.

With each stage, your body should come closer to the floor. In the last stage, your chest and stomach should rest on the floor with the lower area of the back slightly arched.

Concentration

Waist, lower back, hips, inner thighs and legs

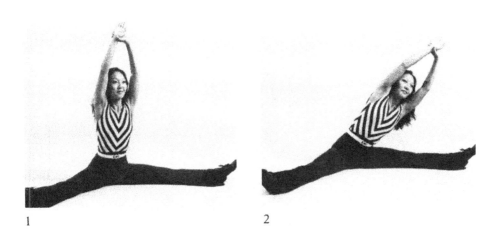

1   2

SPREAD LEG STRETCH

3

4

5

6

SPREAD LEG STRETCH

7

8

9

10

SPREAD LEG STRETCH

Variation 1

2

3

SPREAD LEG STRETCH

4

5

6

SPLIT PREPARATION STRETCH

Starting Position

Kneel down supporting yourself on your left knee and right foot. Your hands are at your waist. The back is straight and the head erect.

Description

Keeping the right foot flat, slowly rock forward, bending the right knee beyond the toe. Your left leg will begin to straighten. Try to press your left thigh parallel to the ground. Hold, then return to the starting position. Slowly shift your weight backwards, bending the left knee and straightening the right leg. Do not let your buttocks rest on your rear leg Now reach forward with your chin and chest over the right extended leg. Your arms reach out towards your toes. Return to the starting position and repeat switching legs.

Breathing

Normal, regulated breathing.

Posture

While leaning forward in the starting position, keep your back as straight as possible. When reaching forward over the extended leg, your back should be flat.

Remarks

Move into the forward and backwards leaning position slowly. Do not drop your body. For a greater stretch, when bending the right leg and straightening the left knee, begin pushing the left leg backwards.

This exercise is a preliminary training aid for achieving a full splits position, (see Advanced Exercises)

Concentration

Hips, hamstrings and legs.

SPLIT PREPARATION STRETCH

1

2

3

SPLIT PREPARATION STRETCH

4

5

6

INNER THIGH STRETCH

Starting Position

Assume the horse stance, the hands are outstretched and the palms are facing down.

Description

Lean to the right, looking towards the left knee. Seventy percent of your weight is now on your right leg. Bend at the waist, leaning over the left side. Your chest is facing forward with your head aligned with your body. Reach with your right hand over your head while your left arm pulls across the front of your body towards the right side. As you bring the body up, your arms cross in front of yourself returning to the outstretched position. Shift your weight to your left leg while straightening out your right leg. Repeat, stretching to the right side.

Breathing

Inhale in the starting position. Exhale while leaning to the sides.

Posture

Keep the back straight and head aligned with the body when stretching to the sides. Your feet must remain flat and hips tucked under throughout the entire exercise.

Remarks

When stretching sideways over each leg; reach out with your upper body. Try to bend the knees into a low stance to increase the degree of stretch. The upper body must remain relaxed.

Variation

Reach over the bent leg and attempt to bring your side to the knee. Lower the body by bending more each time.

Concentration

Waist, hips, inner thighs and legs.

INNER THIGH STRETCH

1

2

3

INNER THIGH STRETCH

4

5

6

INNER THIGH STRETCH

7

Variation 1   2

TWISTING THIGH STRETCH

Starting Position

Assume the square horse with the back straight and the head erect. The arms are extended with palms facing towards the floor.

Description

Lean to the right side locking the left knee. Seventy percent of your weight is now on your right leg. Turn at the waist to the left side as far as possible. Hold at the point of maximum stretch. Return to the starting position. Twist as far as possible to the right side. Hold, then return to the starting position. Repeat with the left knee bent and the right leg extended.

Breathing

Normal, regulated breathing.

Posture

Keep your back straight, hips tucked under and feet flat throughout the exercise. Keep your head aligned with your body.

Remarks

The bent leg must carry at least seventy percent of your weight. As your legs become stronger, begin shifting more weight onto the bent leg. Keep your back straight when you are twisting. Do no lean forward. Practice the exercise at a slow pace.

Concentration

Waist, hips, lower back, thighs, inner thighs and legs.

TWISTING THIGH STRETCH

1

2

3

4

TWISTING THIGH STRETCH

5

6

7

8

HIP STRETCH

Starting Position
Kneel on both knees which are spread about shoulder width apart. The feet are turned on the insteps. The back is straight and the hips are tucked under the body.

Description
Slowly push the knees out away from the body. Lower your arms to the floor in front of your body to hold it up. Try to spread the legs out as far as possible. Gently rock forwards and backwards.

Breathing
Normal, regulated breathing.

Posture
Keep your head in alignment with the body. Your hips should remain tucked under your body throughout the entire exercise.

Remarks
You will probably feel a little strain in the groin area. Be sure you have warmed up before practicing this exercise and keep your rocking motion very gentle. It is easy to pull these groin muscles if the movement is too jerky.

Concentration
Hips, inner thigh and groin.

HIP STRETCH

1

2

3

4

COBRA STRETCH

Starting Position

Lie on your stomach with your hands at your sides, fingers facing forward and your head turned to the side.

Description

Inhale, then exhale and push your upper body until your arms are fully extended. Just before your elbows are locked straight, turn the hands until the fingers are pointing in slightly. Bend your head back as far as possible and keep your hips on the floor. Hold at the point of maximum stretch of the abdominal muscles. Inhale and lower your body to the ground with the arms returning to the starting position.

Breathing

Inhale before starting the stretch. Exhale while pushing the upper body up. Inhale as you lower your body to the ground.

Remarks

Be sure to look up with your head bent back when your arms are extended. Pay close attention to correct breathing during the exercise.

This exercise should be used to stretch out the abdominals after any exercise which places a strain in this particular area.

Concentration

Lower back and abdominal muscles.

COBRA STRETCH

1

2

3

4

LOWER BACK STRETCHES

Starting Position

Lie on your stomach with your head resting on your crossed hands. Your legs are extended straight out behind you with your toes pointed.

Description

Slowly lift your right leg off the ground. Both hips and upper body remain on the ground and the leg remains straight. Hold, then slowly lower to the ground. Repeat with the left leg and then repeat this series alternating the legs. Slowly lift both legs from the ground keeping the hips and upper body on the ground. Lower and repeat.

Breathing

Inhale, then exhale while lifting the legs. Inhale while lowering the legs.

Posture

Keep your back straight and the hips and upper body should remain on the ground. Keep your legs straight while lifting.

Remarks

Keep the body as relaxed as possible. Only the lower back should feel slightly stressed while lifting each leg.

Variation

Slightly raise the upper body using only the abdominals. Then lift each leg, keeping the upper body raised. Lower the upper body and legs at the same time.

Concentration

Lower back, abdominals and legs.

LOWER BACK STRETCHES

1

2

3

LOWER BACK STRETCHES

4

5

6

LOWER BACK PRESS

Starting Position

Lie on your back, the knees are bent, the legs pressed together and the feet are flat on the floor. Your hands rest on your stomach.

Description

Raising the head up to bring your chin to your chest, press the lower back into the floor. Hold, tightening your abdominal muscles. Lower your head to the floor and repeat.

Breathing

Inhale while lying on the floor. Exhale while pressing your lower back into the floor.

Posture

Keep your legs together and feet flat throughout the entire exercise. Your hands should remain off the floor. Do not use them to press your back into the floor.

Remarks

Relax your body as much as possible. Do not raise your shoulders— only your head lifts up. Try to hold this pressing position as long as possible. If you feel that your lower back is not fully pressing into the floor, tightening your legs will help. It is preferable, however, to keep your legs relaxed as much as possible.

Concentration

Lower back and abdominals.

LOWER BACK PRESS

1

2

ADVANCED STRETCHING EXERCISES

FOOT BEHIND NECK

Starting Position

Sit on the floor with the legs together, the back straight and the head erect.

Description

Bend the right knee and grab the right ankle with both hands. Pull your foot towards your chest and hold at the point of maximum stretch. Reach underneath the foot with your right hand so that the right arm can help in lifting with the outer left arm. Slowly lift the foot to your nose without bending your back and hold at the point of maximum stretch.

Continue by slowly pulling the foot to your ear. Keep your back straight and do not turn you head. Hold at the point of maximum stretch.

From that position, pull your foot in front of your face and over the top of your head. Hold at the point of maximum stretch.

Slowly lower the foot, returning to the starting position. Repeat with the left foot.

Posture

The back is straight and the head is erect throughout the entire exercise. One leg will always remain extended throughout the exercise. Shoulders should be relaxed.

Breathing

Normal, regulated breathing.

Remarks

Move the leg very slowly and be sure you are warmed up before starting the exercise. If you cannot fully reach any of the positions, stretch as far as you can. For example, if you cannot bring your foot to your ear, bring it as close as you can without turning the head or bending the back.

Variation

After bringing the foot to the position above the head, slowly lower it behind your neck. Slowly lift the head and arch the back as much as possible. This is an advanced stretch! It takes time and patience to achieve this level.

Concentration

Lower back, hips, hamstrings, groin and inner thighs.

FOOT BEHIND NECK

1

2

3

4

FOOT BEHIND NECK

5

6

7

LEG LIFT AND PULL

Starting Position

Sit on the floor with the legs extended and the toes pointed. Your back is straight and your head is erect.

Description

Keeping your back straight slowly lift the right leg. Grabbing the ankle with both hands, slowly pull it up to the body as far as possible. Hold at the point of maximum stretch. Then, slowly flex your foot until the bottom of the foot is parallel to the ceiling. Then, point your toes until the foot is in line with the leg. Repeat flexing and pointing several times. The last position should be with the toes pointed. Release the leg and, with your hands on your waist, slowly return the leg to the floor. Repeat with the other leg.

Breathing

Normal, regulated breathing.

Posture

It is important to keep your back straight and head erect. Do not lean backwards. The other leg should remain extended straight out.

Remarks

If you cannot reach the ankle when grabbing the leg, you may grab the calf. If you are very flexible, try holding the heel as a new challenge.

When pointing and flexing your foot, move very slowly and avoid jerky motions. Also be certain that the leg is locked.

Be sure to control the movement of the leg after completing the exercise. Do no lean backwards and do not drop it to the floor.

Variation

Roll onto your left side, propping your upper body on the left elbow. Lift your right leg up as far as possible. Grasp the ankle and slowly pull the leg behind your head as far as possible. Alternate, flexing and pointing your foot from this position. Release the leg and slowly lower it to the starting position. Repeat with the other leg.

Concentration

Lower back, hips, hamstring, groin, thigh, calf, shin, ankle and lower abdominals.

LEG LIFT AND PULL

1

2

3

4

LEG LIFT AND PULL

Variation 1

2

3

4

STANDING LEG EXTENSION

Starting Position

Stand with the feet together, the back straight, the head erect, and the hands at your waist.

Description

Shifting your weight onto your left leg, bend your right knee and lift it to waist level. Grab the ankle with both hands and pull your foot up to your stomach.

Return your left hand to your waist and grasp the instep of your right foot with your right hand. Slowly extend the leg to the side until the leg is locked. Slowly pull the leg into your body and hold at the point of maximum stretch. Bend the knee and return the foot back to the bent position. Repeat and return to the starting position. Repeat the exercise with the other leg.

Breathing

Normal, regulated breathing.

Posture

Keep your standing leg locked. Do not lean sideways or forward as you pull the leg up.

Remarks

This exercise requires excellent balance and, in the beginning, you may wish to extend your arm as a counterweight or support yourself on a nearby wall (but do not lean heavily or depend on the wall).

As you extend the leg out, it is important to relax as much as possible. Do not overstretch the leg if the extension puts severe tension in the groin area and hamstring muscles. Each time you tuck and repeat, try to stretch the leg a bit further.

Concentration

Hips, groin, hamstring and inner thighs.

STANDING LEG EXTENSION

1

2

3

STANDING LEG EXTENSION

4

5

6

CHINESE SPLITS PREPARATION

Starting Position

Kneeling with the knees separated. The back is straight and the head is erect.

Description

Extend the right leg directly to the side of the body, keeping the foot on the floor. Your arms are extended in front of you, bracing your body on the floor. Slowly slide the extended leg out as far as possible. Hold at the point of maximum stretch. Turn your upper body towards the extended leg and slowly lower it, attempting to rest your chest on the leg. Your right arm braces your body behind the extended leg. Pull your body up and return to the starting position. Repeat on the other side.

Breathing

Normal, regulated breathing.

Posture

Make sure your extended leg is in line with your tucked leg and the hips are tucked under your body.

Remarks

As this exercise puts pressure on the bent knee, you may wish to cushion it with a towel or pillow to avoid bruising it. If your ankles are tight, you may wish to turn the foot of the extended leg.

This exercise works on the inner thigh so you should be warmed up before attempting it. Be sure to practice the exercise slowly, particularly when bending towards the extended leg.

Concentration

Hips, groin, inner thigh and ankles.

CHINESE SPLITS PREPARATION

1

2

3

PHOENIX STRETCH

Starting Position
The feet are together, the back is straight, and the head is erect.

Description
Turn the left foot at a forty-five degree angle. Step forward with the right leg until it is a foot in front of the body and in line with the heel of the left leg. Bend the left knee shifting your weight onto the rear leg. Put your right foot on its heel with the toes pointing up. Reach down and grab your foot with both hands. Pull your head towards your toes. Hold at the point of maximum stretch. Slowly raise your body up. Shift your weight onto the right leg while bending the knee. Pivot your upper body to the left leg and repeat the stretch.

Breathing
Normal, regulated breathing.

Posture
Be sure to keep your back leg bent and the front leg locked. The body should remain extended while stretching over the front leg.

Remarks
Be sure your legs are warmed up before attempting this stretch. When reaching over the extended leg, slightly arch the lower area of the back. Try to bring the upper area of your body parallel to the extended leg. Keep your hips tucked in under your body.

In the beginning, you may grab your calf or ankle. As you become more flexible, hold your heel. Eventually you will be able to touch your chin to your toes.

Variation
Once you are ready to pivot to your other leg, do not bring your body all the way up; instead, roll at the waist as you turn.

Concentration
Lower back, hips, hamstrings, ankles and back of knees.

PHOENIX STRETCH

1

2

3

4

ADVANCED SPLITS

Starting Position

The feet are separated with the right leg forward, the left leg back, the back is straight and the head erect. The hands are extended to the sides.

Description

Slowly slide the legs out lowering yourself into a splits position. Turn over the left foot until it is resting on the instep. Hold at the point of maximum stretch. Eventually, you will be flat on the ground. Return to the starting position.

Breathing

Normal, regulated breathing.

Posture

It is important to keep your back straight and the legs straight.

Remarks

Be sure you are warmed up before attempting this exercise. You should concentrate on controlling the movement of the muscles as well as stretching them. Do not try to hyperextend your muscles. Just drop as low as you can and hold. Do not drop yourself quickly, but execute the exercise very, very slowly.

Practicing this exercise in conjunction with the preparation for the splits exercise will soon give you a very advanced degree of flexibility.

Variation

In the starting position, lower yourself a few inches. Hold and pivot at the hips until you are facing the opposite direction. Your feet should pivot also. Lower yourself a few more inches, hold and pivot in the reverse direction. Continue pivoting and lowering until you reach the ground. This will intensify the stretch of the hip areas.

Concentration

Hips, groin, hamstrings, front and back of the thighs and ankles.

ADVANCED SPLITS

i

2

Variation 1

ADVANCED SPLITS

2

3

4

EXERCISES WITH A PARTNER

SIT UPS WITH PARTNER

Starting Position

Sit on the floor with your legs extended and your hands on your stomach. Your partner will be facing you also with extended legs. Place your feet on the outside of your partner's feet.

Description

Press your partner's feet between your feet. Slowly, you and your partner should lower the upper parts of your bodies to just above the floor. Return to the starting position. Switch foot positions with your partner and repeat.

Posture

Keep your legs locked, back straight and your head in alignment with your body. Your shoulders should be relaxed throughout the entire exercise.

Breathing

Inhale while lowering your body. Exhale while raising your body.

Remarks

Press firmly on your partner's feet. This will work on your legs and abdominal muscles and, at the same time, keep your partner's feet from rising from the ground during the situp.

Be sure your legs are kept locked and your feet are flexed during the entire exercise.

Variation

Instead of pressing both your partner's feet, press only the left foot between your feet, while your partner presses your left foot. Lower and raise your body in a situp and then alternate so you are pressing your partner's right foot between both your feet and your partner is pressing your right foot only.

Concentration

Upper and lower abdominals, thighs, knees, calves, shins and ankles.

SIT UPS WITH PARTNER

1

2

3

SIT UPS WITH PARTNER

4

5

6

LEG PRESS WITH PARTNER

Starting Position

Sit on the floor with your hands on your waist, the legs are extended with your back straight and your head erect. Your partner will be facing you with his legs extended. Place your feet on the outside of your partner's feet.

Description

Tensing the legs as much as possible, try to press your partner's feet together. At the same time, your partner should try to separate the feet. Hold for five seconds, then relax. Repeat the exercise with your feet on the inside and with your partner's feet on the outside.

Posture

Keep your back straight, head erect, and legs extended throughout the entire exercise.

Breathing

Inhale while pressing. Exhale while relaxing.

Remarks

Do not lean forward or backwards to compensate for the tension. All tension should be concentrated in your legs and lower abdominals. Keep your feet flexed and upper body relaxed. Do not be concerned if your heels rise slightly during the exercise.

Variations

Practice the exercise with your toes pointed.

Concentration

Lower abdominals, thighs (especially inner thigh), knees, shins, calves, ankles and feet.

LEG PRESS WITH PARTNER

1

2

3

LEG PRESS WITH PARTNER

4

5

6

GROIN STRETCH WITH PARTNER

Starting Position

Sit on the floor with your back straight and your head erect. Separate your legs as far apart as possible. Your partner will be facing you with his/ her legs separated and feet placed on the inside of your ankles.

Description

Hold your partner's hands. Your partner begins lying back pulling your upper body forward and stretching your groin and inner thigh muscles by pushing against your ankles at the same time. Hold at the point of maximum stretch. From this position, your partner bends at the waist to the left. This stretches your right side to your right leg. Then your partner bends at the waist to the right, stretching your left side to your left leg. Return to the starting position and switch positions with your partner.

Posture

Keep your legs extended and knees locked throughout the entire exercise. Your upper body and shoulders should be relaxed. Your back is stretched forward as far as possible when your partner is pulling you.

Breathing

Normal and regulated breathing.

Remarks

Make sure you are warmed up before trying this exercise. Let your partner know how far you can be pulled forward and sideways to avoid pulling any muscles. The stretch should be performed very slowly—never jerk your partner's body. If you are not sufficiently stretched with your partner's feet at your ankles, have your partner move the feet to about mid-calf.

Variation

Your partner first stretches your body to the right side, then to the center, then to the left before returning to the starting position, making the exercise a continuous rolling action.

Concentration

Hips, inner thighs, groin, backs of the knees, waist and lower back.

GROIN STRETCH WITH PARTNER

1

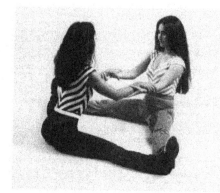

2

3

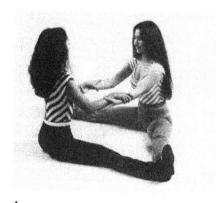

4

GROIN STRETCH WITH PARTNER

5

6

7

8

SPLIT STRETCH WITH PARTNER

Starting Position

    Lie flat on the ground with the legs pressed together, toes pointed and hands at your sides.

Description

    Lift your right leg with toes pointed as high as possible. Kneeling at your side your partner presses your left thigh to hold your leg on the ground while pushing your extended leg towards your chest. Hold at the point of maximum stretch. As your partner releases you, return to the starting position and stretch the left leg.

Posture

    Keep your back on the floor and both legs extended throughout the stretch.

Breathing

    Normal and regulated breathing.

Remarks

    Make sure you are warmed up before trying this exercise and try to stay as relaxed as possible throughout the entire movement. Your partner must hold your leg on the floor at the thigh and not too near the knee. Be sure to tell your partner when to stop to avoid pulled muscles.

Variation

    Repeat the exercise with the foot flexed.

Concentration

    Hips, hamstrings, groin and the back of the knee.

SPLIT STRETCH WITH PARTNER

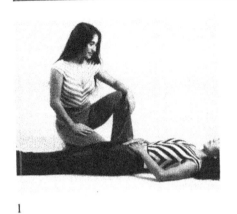

1

2

3

4

EXERCISE WITH A STICK

STICK EXERCISES

To practice these exercises you will need a hardwood dowl approximately one and a half inches in diameter and eighteen inches long. This is available at any lumber yard or hardware store. You may also use a broom handle with the ends cut off. In the beginning stages, many of these exercises can be practiced with a hand towel instead of a stick.

ONE HAND TWIST

Starting Position

Stand with feet together and your back straight. Hold the stick in both hands in front of your body.

Description

Bend your elbows. Turn your right wrist so your palm faces away from the body, and grab the stick. Extend the right arm until it is locked in front of the body. By bending your left wrist in each direction, put pressure on the twisted right wrist flexing it in both directions as well.

Return to starting position and repeat with the left hand.

Breathing

Normal, regulated breathing.

Posture

Relax your shoulders, keep your back straight and legs locked.

Remarks

Try to keep a firm grip with the twisted hand while it is being flexed. Keep the elbow of the twisted hand locked. Relax as much as possible and keep the shoulders as loose as possible.

Concentration

Shoulders, biceps, triceps, elbows and wrist.

ONE HAND TWIST

1

2

3

4

INSIDE OUT WRIST STRETCH

Starting Position

Stand with your feet together and your back straight. Hold the stick with both hands extended in front of yourself.

Description

Bend your elbows, turn your right wrist so your palm faces away from the body and grab the stick from this position. Holding the stick with your right hand, turn your left wrist in the same way and grab the stick again.

Holding the stick with both twisted hands, pull it in front of your chest. Slowly press the stick down until your arms are extended. Bend your wrists to bring the stick towards your body. Hold, then relax and pull your hands back in front of your chest. Slowly push the arms out until they are extended in front of the body. Again, bend your wrists to bring the stick towards you. Hold, then relax and bring your arms back in front of your chest. Repeat the series of movements.

Breathing

Normal, regulated breathing.

Posture

Keep your shoulders relaxed and your back straight.

Remarks

If your wrists are tight and you cannot fully extend your arms, press down as far as possible. Keep your upper body as relaxed as possible.

As you become more flexible in this exercise, begin to bring your hands closer together on the stick.

A towel can be used in the beginning stages of practice; however, keep the towel tight—there should be no slack in the towel as you extend the arms.

Variations

1. When you have extended your arms with wrists twisted, pull your arms straight up over your head. Return them to the front of your body and then pull them up to your chest.
2. Cross your twisted right hand over your twisted left hand. This increases the tension on the shoulders and wrists.

Concentration

Biceps, triceps, elbows, shoulders and wrists.

INSIDE OUT WRIST STRETCH

1

2

3

INSIDE OUT WRIST STRETCH

4

5

6

INSIDE OUT WRIST STRETCH

Variation 1

2

3

4

ELBOW PRESS

Starting Position

Stand with your feet together, back straight and head erect.

Description

Hold the stick between your elbows, arms locked and extended in front of you. Pressing the elbows into the stick, raise both hands overhead. The stick should be lifted over and behind the head. Return to starting position.

Breathing

Normal, regulated breathing.

Posture

Shoulders should be relaxed, the arms locked and the head straight.

Remarks

Put just enough pressure on the stick to keep it from falling. Do not press so hard that you are unable to relax your shoulders. Practice this exercise slowly. Even if you cannot bring the stick behind your head, at least, try to bring it above your head.

Variations

Once the stick is behind your head, lean backwards and to each side carefully and slowly. Be careful not to put too much pressure on the sides of the ribs. Look back with the head while executing this movement.

Concentration

Shoulders, upper body and arms.

ELBOW PRESS

ELBOW PRESS

Variation 1

2

3

KNEE PRESS

Starting Position

Stand with your feet shoulder width apart, back straight and your head erect.

Description

Bend the knees and place the stick between the knees. Apply enough pressure to keep the stick from falling. With hands on your waist, bend forward. Try to bring your head below the level of the stick. Return your upper body to the erect position. Then, slowly lean back. Return to the starting position and repeat.

Breathing

Normal, regulated breathing.

Posture

Keep your hips tucked under your body, your back straight and your feet flat on the ground throughout the entire exercise.

Remarks

It is particularly important to keep your hips tucked under because any arch in your back will strain your lower back muscles. For this reason, when you arch backwards, move very slowly and carefully. Because of your position, you will not be able to move very far backwards. A slight backwards bend is sufficient for this exercise. Make sure the stick is not too near the knee cap.

Concentration

Lower back, abdominals, thighs, knees and buttocks.

KNEE PRESS

1

2

3

4

SHOULDER ROLL

Starting Position

Stand with your feet together, back straight, head erect and arms extended in front of yourself holding the stick with both hands.

Description

Bend the elbows, retaining your hold on the stick. Swing the right hand across your body towards the left shoulder. Turn your wrist so your hand faces your body. Bring your left arm under your right elbow. The stick is now parallel to your side in line with your right shoulder. From this position, bring the stick behind your neck. Your right arm comes down over your face with the right elbow resting on the left elbow. Hold, then pull the right elbow down through the bent left arm and bring the left arm over your head. You should now be in the starting position. Repeat in the opposite direction.

Breathing

Normal, regulated breathing.

Posture

Relax your shoulders and upper body. Keep your back straight and do not lean forward during the exercise.

Remarks

Be sure you have warmed up with various arm stretches before practicing this exercise. In the beginning, you may hear a grinding or popping sound in your shoulders. This is normal and should disappear as you gain in flexibility.

Keep a firm grip on the stick throughout the exercise. A towel can be used in the beginning stages.

SHOULDER ROLL

Variations

Once the stick is behind your neck, begin pulling the stick down your back as far as possible. Return to the position behind the neck and continue with the exercise.

Concentration

Shoulders, upper back, pectorals, front of chest, wrists, elbows and laterals.

1

2

SHOULDER ROLL

3

4

5

6

SHOULDER ROLL

7

8

Variation 1

2

EXERCISES WITH A WEIGHTED TIN CAN

TIN CAN EXERCISES

To make this unusual but very useful piece of equipment, you will need a large, empty, coffee can (or any other type of large tin can) approximately eight inches high. Buy, beg or borrow some dry cement which can also be purchased at a lumber yard or hardware store. Following the instructions, fill the can with cement and let it dry well. Each exercise will indicate whether any other sort of equipment may be substituted for the weighted tin can.

SIT UPS WITH LEG PRESS

Starting Position

Sit with your back straight and your legs extended straight out in front of your body. The weighted can is placed between the feet and your hands on your waist or crossed over your stomach.

Description

Press your feet on the sides of the can. You should feel tension in your inner legs. Slowly lower the upper body, keeping your legs locked and your head in alignment with the body. Lower your body as far as possible without touching the ground. Return to the sitting position. Repeat.

Breathing

Inhale as you lower your body. Exhale as you raise your body.

Posture

Keep your legs locked and feet flexed with your toes up. Keep your head in alignment with your body at all times.

Remarks

Keep steady pressure on the can with your feet.
As you lower your upper body, you will be exercising the lower abdominals. If you wish, you may slightly tip your head back to increase the stretch of the front of the body. Keep the upper portion of your body as relaxed as possible. Use your breathing to help raise and lower your body.
Use any hard object, such as a base of a chair or a waste paper can, instead of a weighted can for this exercise.

Variation

Turn at the waist extending your left arm towards your toes and your right arm behind you. Inhale and lower the body. Keep your arms parallel to the ground. Exhale as you return to the sitting position. Bring your arms forward in front of your body and repeat turning in the opposite direction.

Concentration

Lower back, upper and lower abdominals, thighs, calves and ankles.

SIT UPS WITH LEG PRESS

1

2

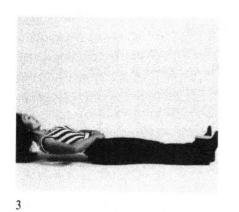

3

4

WEIGHTED LEG LIFTS

Starting Position

Sit with the legs extended and the feet flexed. Place your hands on your waist or in your lap. Your back is straight and head erect. Place the can on top of your ankles.

Description

Tighten your legs while trying to lift the can. At least try to raise your heels from the floor. Hold at the point of maximum tension and relax, bringing your legs down. Repeat.

Breathing

Inhale as you lift the legs. Exhale while relaxing the legs.

Posture

Keep your back straight and head in alignment with your body. Your legs are extended and locked.

Remarks

Do not lean forward or backwards when lifting your legs. Keep the upper portion of your body as relaxed as possible.

Do not be discouraged if you are not lifting your legs at all in the beginning stages. Attempting the exercise, in itself, is an excellent strengthening movement for your muscles. Any heavy object can be used in place of this can for this exercise.

Variation

Lie flat on the floor with the can on your ankles. Your hands are crossed over your chest or placed on your stomach. As you slowly raise your legs, lift your head from the floor. Hold at the point of maximum tension and return your legs to the floor.

Concentration

Lower back, thighs, calves, knees, ankles and lower abdominals.

WEIGHTED LEG LIFTS

1

2

3

HOLDING THE CAN

Starting Position

Sit on the floor with the legs extended about shoulder width apart. The back is straight and the head is erect. Hold the can in front of your chest.

Description

Raise the can over your head with the arms locked. Pointing your toes, slowly lift your legs off the floor. Keeping your arms and head in alignment with the body, slightly lean back as you lift your legs. Lower your legs to the floor and repeat, raising and lowering them.

Breathing

Inhale while sitting. Exhale while lifting the legs.

Posture

Head and arms are in alignment with the body. Keep your legs extended and your toes pointed.

Remarks

Raise the legs slowly but do not try to raise them more than six inches off the ground. Be sure to hold onto the can and keep your arms locked. If it is hard to hold the weight in the beginning, bend your elbows slightly. Keep the weight of the can in line with your head. Your shoulders should be relaxed throughout the exercise. Any heavy object can be substituted for the weighted can.

Concentration

Arms, wrists, hands, lower back, abdominals and legs.

HOLDING THE CAN

1

2

3

4

LEG CLAP

Starting Position

Sit on the floor, the feet are shoulder width apart and your hands are on your waist or in your lap. Your back is straight and your head is erect. Place the can directly between your feet.

Description

Keeping the head in line with the body and the back straight, lean back slightly. Raise both legs above the can and clap them together. Separate and return them to the ground. Repeat.

Breathing

Inhale in the starting position. Exhale while lifting and clapping your feet. Inhale as you return to the starting position.

Posture

Keep your legs straight and head in line with the body. Keep the back straight.

Remarks

Practice this exercise with a slow, controlled motion. If you cannot clap your legs over the can, raise them, at least, to the level of the can and hold them. Keep your upper body relaxed. Your feet may be pointed or flexed for this exercise.
When leaning back slightly, do not allow the lower back to sag.

Variation

After lifting and clapping, lower the legs, do not rest, repeat the exercise without touching the ground.

Concentration

Lower back, lower abdominals, thighs, calves and ankles.

LEG CLAP

1

2

3

KNEE PRESS

Starting Position

Sit on the floor, legs separated, with the can upright between the knees. Your hands are at your waist or in your lap. The back is straight and the head erect.

Description

Keeping your upper body relaxed, press on the sides of the can with your legs. Try to push your feet together. Hold at the point of maximum tension and relax.

Breathing

Exhale while pressing on the can. Inhale, then breathe normally as you relax.

Posture

Keep your legs extended and your back straight.

Remarks

Your feet can be either pointed or flexed for this exercise.

Press as hard as possible so the entire leg will receive the benefits of dynamic tension. The can can be placed just below the knee or slightly above the knee to increase the pressure of the legs.

You can use any other heavy object such as a box, a wastepaper can, a book, etc., in place of the can.

Concentration

Thighs, inner thigh, knees, calves, ankles and lower abdominals.

KNEE PRESS

i

2

3

RAISED SIDE CRUNCH

Starting Position

Lie flat on your left side with both legs propped up on top of the can. Your elbows are bent and your arms are tucked in front of your body.

Description

Using only the waist muscles, bend sideways and raise your upper body off the ground. Your legs remain pressed on the can. Hold at the point of maximum tension. Then, relax and return to the starting position. Repeat on the other side.

Breathing

Inhale while lying on the ground. Exhale while bending at the waist.

Posture

Keep the body in a straight line on its side. Do not tilt forward or backwards. Your legs should remain straight throughout the entire exercise.

Remarks

Your upper body should remain relaxed. Be sure to use only your waist muscles when you bend and lift with a slow controlled motion.

You may cross your feet on the can if you prefer.

Attend to your breathing pattern carefully during this exercise.

Concentration

Waist and hips.

RAISED SIDE CRUNCH

1

2

SIT UPS HOLDING CAN

Starting Position

Sit with your back straight, head erect and legs pressed together. The knees are slightly bent with the feet flat on the floor.

Description

Hold the can in front of your chest with the elbows bent. Slowly lower your upper body as far as possible. Sit up and repeat.

Breathing

Inhale as you lower your body. Exhale as you raise your body.

Posture

Keep your feet flat on the ground and legs pressed together. Your head should remain in alignment with your body and your back is straight.

Remarks

Do not rest the can on your chest, but use your arm strength to hold it. Because of the added weight, be very careful as you lower your body. Do not overstrain your muscles. Keep the body relaxed as much as possible and maintain your breathing. You can use any heavy object such as a small barbell or simply a five pound bag of sugar.

Concentration

Upper and lower abdominals, arms, lower back and the legs.

SIT UPS HOLDING CAN

1

2

3

4

EXERCISES WITH A CHAIR

RAISED INNER THIGH EXERCISE

Starting Position

Lie on your left side. The upper portion of your body is propped up on the left elbow. Extend both legs and rest them on a chair with the right leg on top of the left leg.

Description

Flexing the right foot, raise it until it is perpendicular to the body. Slowly lower it to the floor without resting. Hold for a moment then raise the leg and lower it to the starting position. Repeat this series. Then roll onto your right side and repeat entire exercise.

Breathing

Inhale while raising the leg. Exhale while lowering the leg. Inhale, then exhale while raising the leg again and lowering it to the starting position.

Posture

Keep the body propped up on your left arm. Keep the leg which remains on the chair extended straight throughout the exercise. Do not lean forward or backwards.

Remarks

Make sure you are warmed up before attempting this exercise.

Keep your body relaxed. The leg which is being raised and lowered must stay flexed throughout the entire movement.

In the beginning, when you are lowering your leg in front of your body, you may momentarily rest it on the floor before raising it again.

Use a slow and controlled motion for this exercise. Do not jerk your legs up from the floor or drop them down suddenly.

Concentration

Waist, hips, inner thigh and legs.

RAISED INNER THIGH EXERCISE

1

2

3

4

SIDE CRUNCH WITH A CHAIR

Starting Position

Lie on your left side with both legs extended. Your feet are on the chair with the right leg over left leg. Your arms are tucked in to your chest.

Description

Using only the waist muscles, bend sideways and raise your upper body off the ground. Your legs remain pressed on the chair. Hold at the point of maximum tension for a moment. Then relax and return to the starting position. Repeat on the other side.

Breathing

Inhale while lying on the ground. Exhale while bending at the waist.

Posture

Keep the body in a straight line on your side. Do not tilt forward or backwards. Your legs should remain straight throughout the entire exercise.

Remarks

Your upper body should remain relaxed. Be sure to use only your waist muscles when you bend and lift. Do not jerk to get the upper body off the ground but use controlled movement. Even attempting the exercise will work the waist.

You may cross your feet on the chair if you prefer.

Your breathing pattern will aid in this exercise tremendously.

Concentration

Waist and hips.

SIDE CRUNCH WITH A CHAIR

1

2

LEG CLAPS WITH A CHAIR

Starting Position

Sitting upright in a chair. Do not sit all the way back or rest your back on the back of the chair. Arms rest on the chair, the legs are extended shoulder width apart. Place a second chair between your legs.

Description

Keep your head in alignment with the body and lean back slightly. Point your toes and lift your legs up over the top of the chair. Clap your feet together. Separate your legs and return them to the floor. Repeat.

Breathing

Inhale in the starting position. Exhale while lifting and clapping. Inhale while returning to your original position.

Posture

Keep your legs straight, your head is in alignment with the body and your lower back is straight.

Remarks

Pay close attention to your breathing pattern throughout the exercise. If you cannot clap your feet over the chair, at least, raise them to the level of the chair.
Do not lean backwards further than is necessary to maintain your balance.

Variation

1. Do not touch your feet to the floor in between the lifts.
2. Alternate pointing and flexing your feet with each lift.

Concentration

Lower back, abdominals, hips, thighs and ankles.

LEG CLAPS WITH A CHAIR

1

2

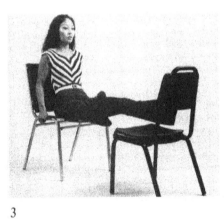
3

4

LEG CLAPS WITH A CHAIR

5

Variation 1

2

3

DOUBLE KNEE LIFTS WITH A CHAIR

Starting Position

Sit upright in the chair with your feet flat on the floor, your hands resting on the chair. Your back is straight and your head erect.

Description

Raise both knees bringing your feet off the floor and pointing your toes. At the same time, push your arms into the chair. Hold at the point of maximum tension, then relax by lowering your feet to the floor again. Repeat.

Breathing

Inhale in the starting position. Exhale while lifting your knees. Inhale while lowering your feet to the ground.

Posture

Keep your back straight and head in alignment with the body. Your knees should be pressed together.

Remarks

Pay close attention to your breathing pattern in this exercise.
As you gain in strength, you will be able to raise your knees higher.
In the beginning, work on controlling your movements. Pushing down with your arms will help you raise your knees higher. Relax your shoulder while pushing into the chair.

Variation

Raise both legs off the ground. Hold the left leg while continuing to raise the right leg. As you lower the right leg, raise the left leg. Alternate pumping the legs without touching the ground.

Concentration

Arms, lower abdominals, thighs, ankles and calves.

DOUBLE KNEE LIFTS WITH A CHAIR

1

2

Variation 1

2

BODY LIFT

Starting Position
Sit in the chair with the feet flat on the ground and the knees together. The back is straight and the head is erect. The hands rest on the chair at the sides of your body.

Description
Keeping the back straight, push down with your arms until they are locked. Lift your body off the chair and hold at the point of maximum tension. Relax by bending your elbows and lowering your body back to the chair. Repeat.

Breathing
Inhale in the starting position. Exhale as you push the body up. Inhale as you lower your body and relax.

Posture
Keep your head in alignment with the body and back straight throughout the exercise. Keep your legs together.

Remarks
When pressing your body up, keep your shoulders relaxed to let your arms do all of the work. Try not to lean forward or backwards.

Although you may not be able to lift the body at first, the tension built up in the arms by this exercise will eventually strengthen them to that point.

Concentration
Arms, upper back, pectorals, lats, wrists and chest.

BODY LIFT

1

2

LEG STRETCH WITH CHAIR

Starting Position

Sit on the floor with the right leg tucked in so the right foot is by the left knee. Put your hands on your waist or in your lap. Extend your right leg straight forward. The back is straight and the head is erect.

Description

Lift your left leg onto the chair with the foot flexed. Pressing the right knee down to the ground, bend forward, reaching with your chin and chest towards the extended leg. Grab the heel of the leg and pull your body forward. Hold at the point of maximum stretch. Relax and return to the starting position.

Turn the body sideways and turn the left leg so it is now resting on its side. Grab your left toe with your right hand. Your left arm reaches over your head to stretch the muscles in your right side. Hold, then return to the starting position.

Turn your body over facing towards the floor and turn your left leg so it is now resting on the instep. Keeping your left leg straight and extended directly behind your arched back, reach backwards with your head. Return to the starting position. Repeat with the other leg.

Breathing

Exhale at the point of maximum stretch. Inhale while relaxing. Maintain normal, regulated breathing during transitions.

Posture

Keep the leg extended on the chair and locked during the series of exercises. Keep your back straight with your head in alignment with your body.

Remarks

Make sure you are warmed up before practicing this exercise. As the leg is elevated, there will be extra tension in the lower back and hips. Do not

LEG STRETCH WITH CHAIR

overstrain yourself.

When stretching sideways, bend at your waist, keeping the upper body relaxed.

When stretching backwards, be careful not to strain the lower back. The back leg must remain locked or you will defeat the purpose of this stretching exercise.

Concentration

Lower back, abdominals, hips, inner thigh, groin, hamstrings, back of the legs and ankles.

1

2

LEG STRETCH WITH CHAIR

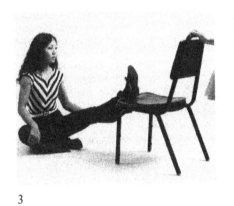

3

4

5

6

LEG SWINGS

Starting Position

Sit upright with the legs together and the hands on a chair. The back is straight and the head is erect.

Description

Lift the right leg as high as possible until it is fully extended; the knee is locked and the toes are pointed. Hold at the point of maximum tension. Slowly swing the extended leg to the left and hold. Then slowly swing it to the right and hold. Repeat the series of swings. Return the leg to the central position and lower it. Repeat with the other leg.

Breathing

Normal and regulated breathing.

Posture

Do not lean while lifting or swinging the leg. Keep the foot of the other leg flat on the floor.

Remarks

When swinging your leg, attempt to move your hip through its full range of motion. This is particularly important when you swing your leg to the side. Try to open the hips fully.

Make sure your swinging is slow and controlled. Do not whip your legs back and forth.

It is essential that your back remains straight. This prevents undue strain being placed on your lower back while focusing the stress on your abdominals and thighs.

Lift your chest to help keep your back straight.

Variation

Repeat the exercise with the feet flexed.

Concentration

Lower back, lower abdominals, thighs, groin, knee, calves and ankle.

The pillow used for the following type of exercises should be compact and firm like a small throw pillow or the cushion used for Zen meditation. As you become more familiar with these exercises, you may improvise and use any handy object such as a book for example.

LEG SWINGS

1

2

3

4

LEG SWINGS

Variation 1

2

3

4

EXERCISES WITH A PILLOW

PILLOW EXERCISES

The pillow used for the following type of exercises should be compact and firm like a small throw pillow or the cushion used for Zen meditation. As you become more familiar with these exercises, you may improve and use any handy object such as a book for example.

LEG TUCKS WITH PILLOW

Starting Position

Sit on the floor with the knees bent and the pillow placed between the knees. The feet are flat on the floor. The back is straight with the hands placed slightly behind the rear and the arms are slightly bent.

Description

Slowly lift your feet off the ground with the toes pointed, tucking your knees to your chest. Your knees should be firmly pressed into the pillow. Slowly extend the right leg until the knee is locked and then hold. Slowly bend it back to the starting position. Repeat, extending with the left leg.

Posture

Knees should be lifted as close to the chest as possible. Keep your lower back straight and head erect throughout the entire exercise.

Breathing

Exhale while extending your leg. Inhale while bending your leg.

Remarks

Maintain steady pressure on the pillow throughout the exercise. The scissoring action should be controlled and slow. Although your hands are bacing yourself, do not lean too far back. In order to keep your back straight, lift your chest and focus on the line where the ceiling and wall meet.

Variations

1. Repeat the exercise with feet flexed.
2. After you have tucked both knees to your chest, extend both legs, maintaining pressure on the pillow. Hold, then return to the tucked position. Be sure to keep your back straight.
3. Repeat the above variation with the feet flexed.

Concentration

Lower back, hips, thighs (especially inner thighs), knees, calves, ankles and lower abdominals.

LEG TUCKS WITH PILLOW

1

2

3

LEG TUCKS WITH PILLOW

4

5

6

BUTTOCKS FIRMER

Starting Position

Lie on your back with the knees bent with the pillow between the knees. The feet are flat on the floor and the hands are on your stomach.

Description

Keeping your feet flat, lift your buttocks slightly off the ground. Begin tightening your buttock muscles, pressing your knees into the pillow at the same time. Continue lifting your buttocks and tightening the muscles further in four counts until your pelvis is in line with your legs. Your body will be flat from your knees to your shoulders. Slowly lower your body and relax your buttock muscles in four counts until you have returned to the starting position and are fully relaxed again.

Posture

Your feet remain flat on the floor with the knees pressed together and the hands remaining on your stomach throughout the entire exercise.

Breathing

Normal, regulated breathing.

Remarks

Make sure you raise and lower your buttocks very smoothly. Irratic movement will strain the lower back.

Variation

Lift the buttocks until your body is in alignment with the shoulders (the highest position in the above exercise) and immediately tighten your muscles as hard as possible. Hold for ten seconds. Lower the buttocks and relax.

Concentration

Abdominals, lower back, inner thighs and buttocks.

BUTTOCKS FIRMER

1

2

3

BUTTOCKS FIRMER

4

5

6

BUTTOCKS FIRMER

7

8

9

LAYERED SIT UPS WITH PILLOW

Starting Position

Sit on the floor with your back straight and head erect. The hands are on the waist and the knees are bent with the feet flat on the floor with the pillow between your knees.

Description

Maintaining a steady pressure on the pillow, lower your upper body halfway to the ground and hold. Then lower your body until it is just above the ground and hold. Slowly raise your body halfway up and hold, then return to the starting position.

Posture

Keep your head in alignment with the body and the back straight. Your shoulders should be relaxed and the feet flat on the ground throughout the exercise.

Breathing

Inhale as you lower your body. Exhale as you raise your body.

Remarks

By pressing the pillow, you double the exertion of the lower abdominal muscles; be sure you can do regular situps easily before attempting this exercise. As this exercise becomes easier for you, increase the pressure on the pillow.

If you are unable to lower yourself to just above the ground, lower yourself as far as your stomach muscles will allow.

Your breathing pattern is very important in this exercise.

Variation

From the starting position, twist your upper body as far as possible to the right. Lower your body halfway, then almost completely to the ground. You should try to bring your rib cage parallel to the floor. Return to the starting position in two stages. Repeat twisting to the left.

Concentration

Upper and lower abdominals, thighs, inner thighs, waist and lower back.

LAYERED SIT UPS WITH PILLOW

1

2

3

4

SUMMARY

There is an ancient Chinese saying, "A woman's beauty is like precious jade." Cosmetics such as lipstick and eye-shadow have been found even in the ancient pyramids of Egypt over thirty-five hundred years ago. Today, in the quest of beauty, women have created a multi-billion dollar cosmetic industry. I believe that today's women want more than just relying on a "painted" face and classy clothes.

Is beauty only skin deep? Of course not! One can reply easily enough but the problem is not in the question but in the answer. How do we become truly beautiful? It is my sincere belief that, in addition to wholesome living, beauty comes from deep inside the woman and is nurtured and cultivated through a glowing sense of health and just simply feeling good about one's self. Beauty, health and self-confidence come, first of all, from being fit and that is why this exercise program is so important. We must take good care of ourselves, not only for our own sake, but for our family and friends as well. Beauty is like a single candle that can light a million others. When I am fit and feel good about myself, my friends and family feel good as well. Isn't this real beauty?

Exercise, keep fit and be beautiful.